TOURING IN WINE COUNTRY

TUSCANY

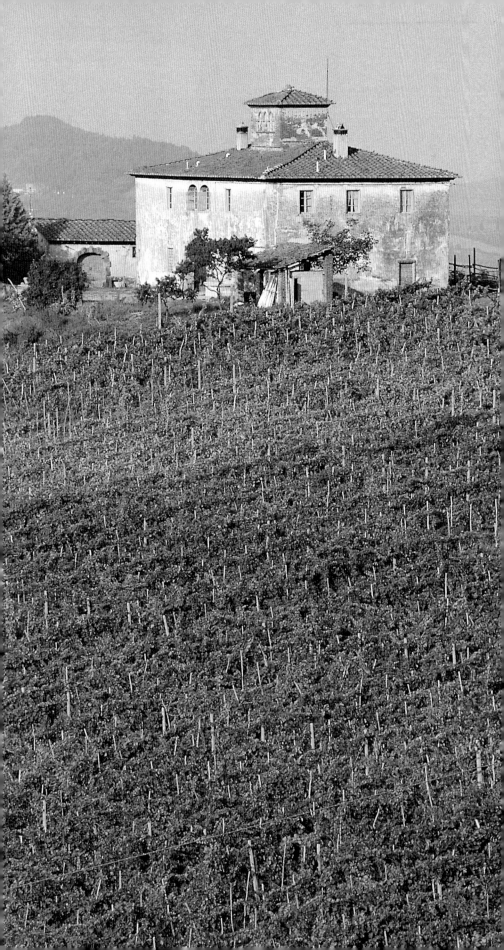

MITCHELL BEAZLEY

TOURING IN WINE COUNTRY
TUSCANY

MAUREEN ASHLEY MW

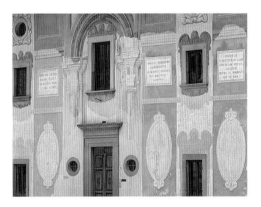

SERIES EDITOR
HUGH JOHNSON

Contents

Touring in Wine Country Tuscany
edited and designed by Mitchell Beazley
an imprint of Octopus Publishing Group
Limited
2-4 Heron Quays, London E14 4JP

First published in 1996
Copyright © Octopus Publishing Group
Limited 1996, 2000
Text copyright © Maureen Ashley
Maps copyright © Octopus Publishing
Group Limited 1996, 2000
All rights reserved

A CIP catalogue record of this book is
available from the British Library

ISBN 1 84000 247 6

Commissioning Editor: Rebecca Spry
Managing Editor: Lucy Bridgers
Index: Angie Hipkin
Gazetteer: Sally Chorley
Cartography: Map Creation Limited
Design by the Bridgewater Book
Company
Illustrations: Polly Raines
Production: Nancy Roberts

Typeset in Bembo and Gill Sans

Printed and bound by Toppan Printing
Company, China

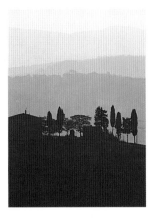

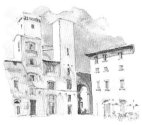

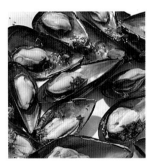

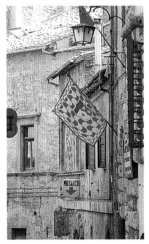

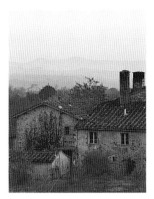

Foreword

Why is it that wine tasted in the cellar (or even in the region) of its birth has a magic, a vibrancy and vigour that makes it so memorable?

It is easy to think of physical reasons. The long journey to the supermarket shelf cannot be without some effect on a living creature - and wine is indeed alive, and correspondingly fragile.

It is even easier to think of romantic reasons: the power of association, the atmosphere and scents of the cellar, the enthusiasm of the grower as he moves from barrel to barrel....

No wonder wine touring is the first-choice holiday for so many people. It is incomparably the best way to understand wine - whether at the simple level of its scenery and culture, or deeper into the subtleties of its terroirs and the different philosophies of different producers.

There are armchair wine-books, coffee-table books, quick reference wine-books...even a pop-up wine book. Now with this series we have the wine-traveller's precise, pin-pointed practical guide to sleuthing through the regions that have most to offer, finding favourites and building up memories. The bottles you find yourself have the genie of experience in them.

Hugh Johnson

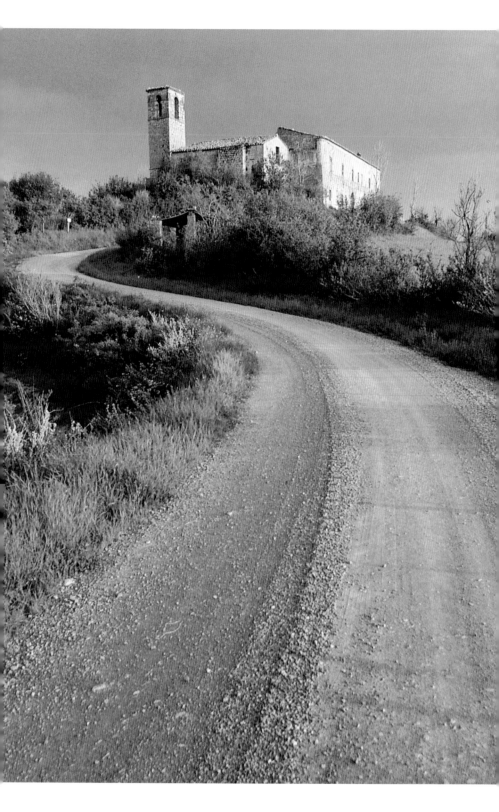

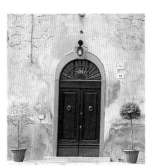

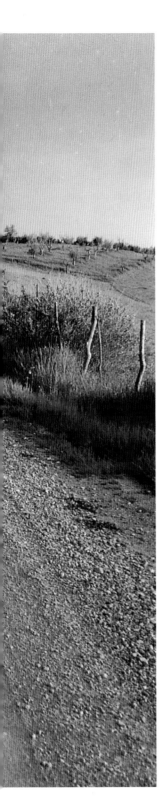

Tuscany

Those who experience sensory overload from the surfeit of artistic wonders in Florence are said to be suffering from Stendhal's syndrome. There is no recognized equivalent for those overwhelmed by Tuscany's natural beauties – but there should be. It is impossible to travel through the region and remain unmoved by its grace, its wildness, its shapes, colours and panoramas. Its variety is enthralling: bare crests give way to pine forests, wheat fields and olive groves, and row after row of neatly tended vines – all punctuated by inspiring villas. Combined with good wine, good food and the Tuscans themselves, it is more than enough to engender a life-time's love-affair.

Tuscany is joyous at any time of year. Spring is wonderful, with almond and cherry blossom, lush green wheat and sprouting vines. In summer, cool hill slopes, fresh coastal breezes and plentiful shade prevent overheating, although August, when most Italians (including city restaurateurs) are on holiday, can be a bit frenetic. Autumn brings renewed tranquillity and the heady aromas of the harvest. Even winter brings compensations: roads are clear; bare vines reveal their carefully pruned forms; mimosa brings a splash of colour and bright, crisp days give incomparable views.

Much of the landscape has been shaped by the region's countless wars and by the *mezzadria*, the old crop-sharing system. Fortified towns and villages were built high with castles on the more commanding positions as a result of continuous battles between rival dukedoms, principalities and city states. The *mezzadria* landowners lived in large, imposing villas surrounded by stables, granaries, wine cellars, oil presses, a chapel and more while the share croppers' small *case coloniche* (farmhouses) dotted their land. As the system broke down, some estates consolidated, bought back land

Left *Travelling through Tuscany raises the spirits and calms the soul whatever the weather.*

Top *A characteristic painted doorway in Montecatini, province of Pistoia.*

from their ex-*mezzadri* (who moved on to more lucrative jobs in the cities) and concentrated on one or two crops rather than the old polyculture. Others fragmented as the peasant farmers bought land, and formed the network of small quality-conscious growers, who have done so much to raise Tuscany's image.

THE ENOTECA

Most towns and many villages sport at least one *enoteca*, or wine shop. Some concentrate on local wines, others stock the more important Tuscan/Italian wines too. Occasionally they can be tasted. Some *enoteche* serve snacks, others place a greater emphasis on food and are more like wine bars.

TRAVELLING AROUND

It is easier to find your way around some provinces than others. There are nine in all, each responsible for its local road signs. Some are more effective than others – in Pisa, for example, you may feel like resorting to a compass. There is a good network of *autostrade* (motorways) and *superstrade* (toll-free) dual-carriageways). Not all are on maps, so follow signs (blue for *autostrade*, green otherwise). If planning to use the *autostrada* system a lot, consider buying a Viacard, a debit card for the tolls. Otherwise avoid this, and residents' credit system lanes, unless you enjoy making Italians irate.

Most town centres are now pedestrianized with well sign-posted car parks around them. Some are pay-and-display, but many of the machines are not yet converted to accept new coinage introduced in 1995, so hang on to any old coins.

The local tourist office will supply much information, but if you cannot find it, try looking for Azienda Provinciale Turismo (APT) in the Yellow Pages under Enti Turistiche.

Note: It is quite common for the electricity to be cut during storms and street lighting can fail. So take a torch.

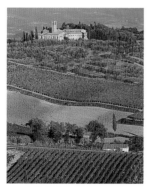

Above *The rolling hills around San Gimignano, where Vernaccia is made into full, dry white wine.*

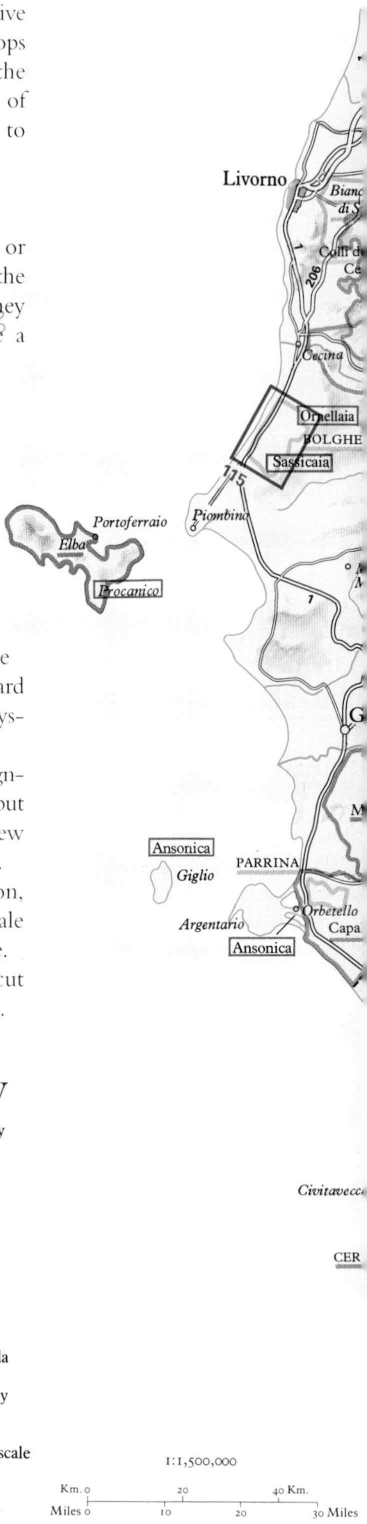

Central Italy

—·—·—	International boundary
—·—·—	Regione boundary
Zagarolo	White wine
Chianti	Red wine
TORGIANO	Red and white wine
VIN SANTO	Dessert wine
Sassicaia	Selected Vino da Tavola

DOC boundaries are distinguished by coloured lines

115	Area mapped at larger scale on page shown
	Land above 600 metres

1:1,500,000

Km. 0   20   40 Km.
Miles 0   10   20   30 Miles

Map labels: Livorno, Bianc di S, Colli d Ce, Cecina, Ornellaia, BOLGHE, Sassicaia, Portoferraio, Piombino, Elba, Procanico, M, G, Ansonica, Giglio, PARRINA, Argentario, Orbetello, Capa, Ansonica, Civitavecc, CER

INTRODUCTION

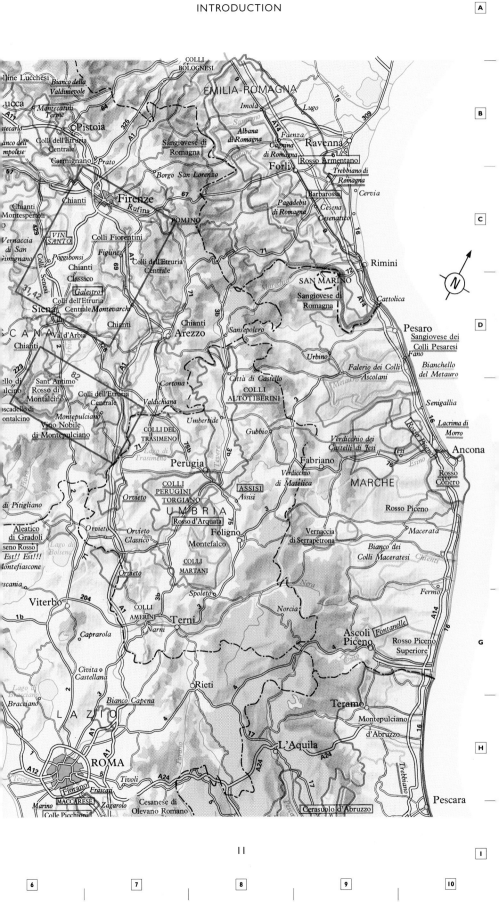

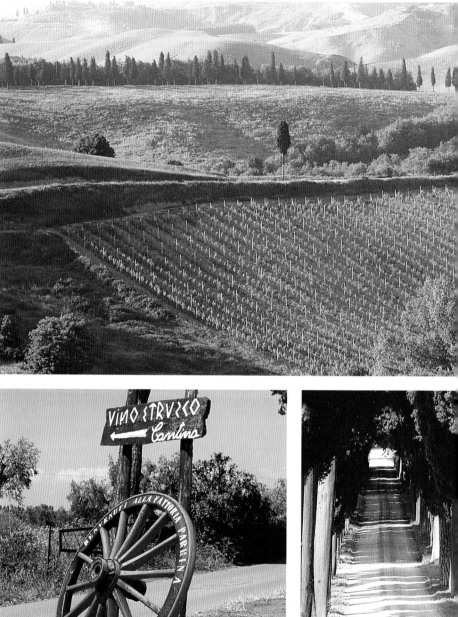

Above *Entrance to the Parrina estate in southwest Tuscany. Visiting Tuscany's wines estates not only unveils the secrets of the wines, but gives a closer understanding of the region as a whole.*

Visiting estates

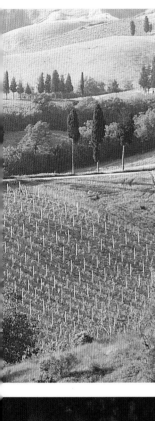

Most Italians are wonderfully hospitable and (winemakers especially) love to talk about their work, so it is seldom difficult to arrange to visit an estate. For most producers, however, making wine is their livelihood, not a hobby or a sideline, and they simply cannot drop everything for an hour or so whenever a passer-by expresses an interest. So it is imperative to telephone first for an appointment. A day or two before is usually enough; more than a couple of weeks may be too long.

It can be hard to arrange a visit around the first weekend of April, as most producers will be at Italy's important wine fair in Verona. January and August are the most common holiday periods. Harvest – late August to mid-October – is an exciting experience, but producers are even more hard-pressed than usual and may have little time for visitors.

Estates vary widely in what they offer. Some give a full tour of vineyards, winemaking and ageing cellars, followed by a tasting. Others may show a video or offer only a tasting. Usually tastings are free. You are not expected to buy anything but it may be courteous to do so. Some estates offer refreshments, even meals. Others produce and sell complementary products such as olive oil and honey.

AGRITURISMO

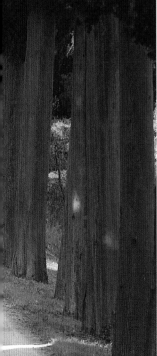

Many estates have set up *agriturismo*, or 'green tourism' ventures, which began as a way of giving townsfolk an insight into country life, but developed into a pleasant, inexpensive way of staying in the Italian countryside. Furnished apartments or rooms in villas on a wine, olive or general farming estate are rented out for a minimum of one week. *Agriturismo* is incredibly popular, however, and apartments need booking well in advance. Standards vary widely too: some are delightful traditional Tuscan farmhouses, well-appointed with swimming pools, others are depressing, so it is best to book through a reliable agency.

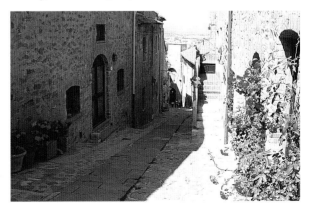

13

Viticulture, vinification and wine law

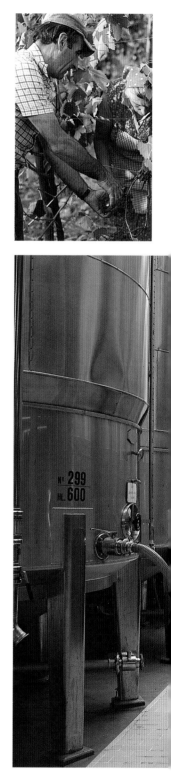

As far as is known, Tuscany has been producing wine since Etruscan times. Nevertheless, it is only in the past decade that the majority of wines have become so exciting. Much of the development has been led by consultants, dedicated men and women with rare skills in extracting the best from each plot of land.

GROWING GRAPES

Whether stretching over tens of hectares or dotted in tiny plots, most Tuscan vineyards are neatly planted on a tidy grid, stretched carefully along wires. Most new plantings now have 4,000 or more vines per hectare, almost twice the previous density. Despite the costs and vastly increased labour, growers have taken the plunge as quality benefits. They have also been careful to replant better-quality clones.

Vines are usually trained low so that they gain reflected warmth from the ground and waste less energy supporting unproductive woody growth. The main training systems are cordon spur, where the trunk of the vine is trained in an inverted L-shape and each season's growth starts from a series of spurs left on the horizontal; and guyot, where the trunk is a stump from which one or two canes from one year's fruiting shoots are trained horizontally to provide those for the next year. Pruning during the vines' winter rest period reforms these shapes and, vitally, restricts growth. Wine laws specify a maximum yield but the best growers aim even lower, sometimes lopping burgeoning bunches to concentrate the quality of the remaining grapes.

The vine's growth starts in early spring, when buds are susceptible to frost damage. A patch of warm weather will see shoots spurt remarkably quickly and keep growers busy attaching the new growth to wires. The vine flowers between late spring and early summer. Fine weather is crucial to ensure a full pollination and avoid malformed or partially formed berries – an annual concern.

During the growing season some growers leave the grasses that spring up around the vines to fix the topsoil, others plough them in for humus, a few treat them with herbicides. As the grape bunches form, growers often trim foliage to improve the grapes' exposure to light and sun. Grapes develop their colour in the month before full ripeness. A little rain is welcome at this point to flesh them out, especially if the summer has been hot and dry.

The harvest itself (which starts in late August for some white varieties and continues into October for reds) needs dry conditions. Wet weather leads to dilution, rot – and profoundly depressed producers.

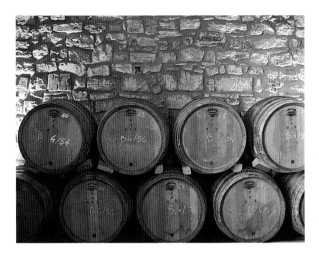

Far left *Picking is still best done by hand to ensure the healthiest grapes are chosen.*
Left *Traditionally Tuscan reds have been aged in large oak casks called* botti. *Recently there has been a trend towards smaller, new oak French* barriques *and producers have been experimenting with woods of different sources and ages.*
Below *Most Tuscan estates have invested in hygienic, stainless steel vats with good temperature control.*

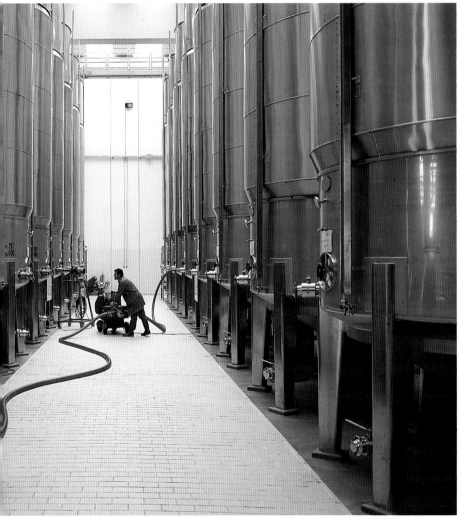

GRAPE VARIETIES

Most Tuscan reds are based on Sangiovese, an excellent variety which can turn out reasonable wine quite easily but is difficult to master. Blending in small quantities of other grapes (often Canaiolo, Mammolo or Ciliegiolo) for extra complexity is common practice. Traditional white grapes are Trebbiano and Malvasia, which need skilful winemaking to give fine wine.

Recent years have seen many experiments in Tuscany with non-traditional varieties, particularly red Cabernet Sauvignon, Merlot and Syrah and the whites Chardonnay and Sauvignon.

MAKING THE WINE

The colour, flavour and tannin in red wine come from the grape skins, so grapes for red wine are first of all crushed, to bring the skins and juice into contact. The skins remain with the juice during fermentation. The winemaker decides the best temperature at which to ferment and how long to leave the juice on the skins. Most Tuscan reds then go into large wooden casks to 'soften' or add a little vanilla-like silkiness. The casks, or *botti,* are usually made from Slovenian oak and are sometimes a century or more old. More recently there has been a trend to use small, new French-oak *barriques*.

The fresh fruitiness of white wines comes from pressing the grapes immediately after picking to separate juice from the skins. The juice is then fermented on its own. Tuscan whites are most often aged in stainless steel; only a few are put into oak. Italians love drinking white wine very young,

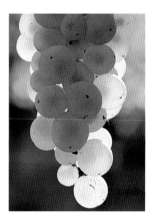

Above *Vernaccia di San Gimignano, which can produce full-bodied, dry wines.*

Below *Sangiovese is often blended with small quantities of other varieties but also makes an excellent wine on its own.*

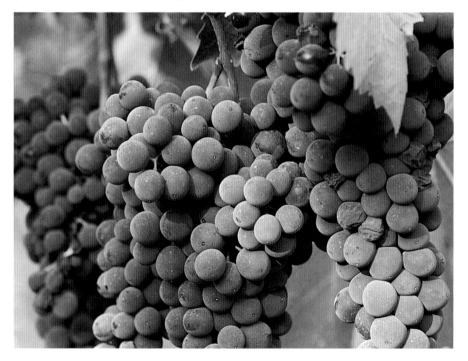

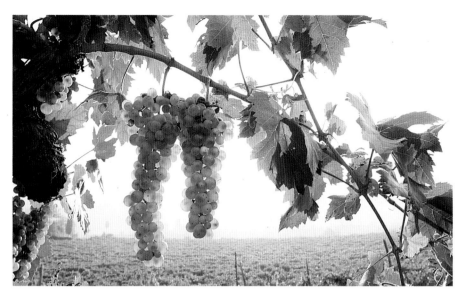

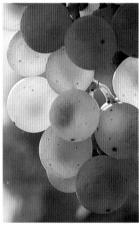

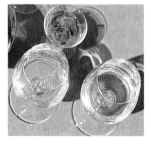

and even the top growers find it hard to resist their customers' demand and sell them ever earlier in the season.

Sweet Vin Santo, or 'Holy wine', is made all over Tuscany from dried raisin-like grapes, whose juice is fermented very slowly in tiny *caratelli* (barrels) containing *madre*, debris from the previous years' wine. The *caratelli* are sealed and left for three years or more before the wine is released and bottled.

WINE CLASSIFICATION

Italy's first wine rules were designed in the early 1960s, with the categories *Vino da Tavola* (VdT, simple 'table wine'), *Denominazione di Origine Controllata* (DOC, 'quality' wines) and DOCG (the 'G' for *e Garantita*, supposedly a super-category starting up in the early 1980s). At this time the Italian wine scene was at its worst: poor practices were rife, and the aim quantity, not quality.

As producers became increasingly experimental and innovative and quality became the industry's ethos, many found DOC(G) constraints a hindrance. Frequently they ignored them, making the best wines they could regardless. Officially just VdT wine, each was given a *nome di fantasia*, prominent on the label. This widespread practice and a few bureaucratic misjudgements brought the wine law into such disrepute that a complete revision was called for. It was published in 1992 and is gradually coming into effect.

Only the most basic wines will now be VdT. A new category, Indicazione Geografica Tipica (IGT) covers broadly regional wine styles, while new, stricter DOC(G)s will be created for sub-zones even as small as individual vineyards. Thus classifications will be nested like a Russian doll and, in any year, wine not up to the standard of the area's tightest DOC(G) may be declassified one or more levels.

Malvasia (top) *and Trebbiano* (centre), *once used in Chianti, are now more commonly made into crisp, dry wine.*

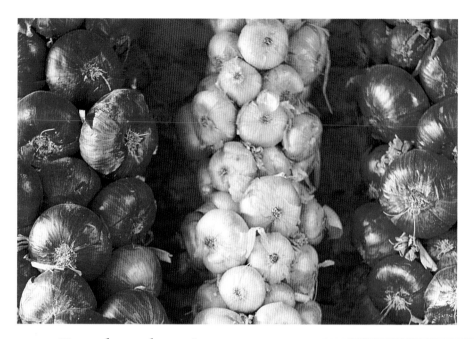

Food and eating out

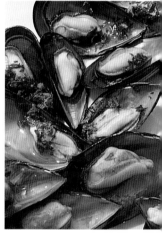

Throughout Tuscany food is wholesome and fairly simple. Olive oil is used liberally and the diet strongly meat-oriented. Bread is firm and unsalted, except for rich, flat *scacciata*. The only variation is along the coast where freshly caught fish naturally predominates, especially in summer.

EATING OUT

You are unlikely to eat badly in Tuscany. Pop into any *trattoria* (avoiding any aimed specifically at tourists, with menus in several languages or spattered with odd English phrases) and the meal will normally be enjoyable. If, as you look in, you see the oil in the cruet is a beautiful deep green colour, you can look forward to the meal with even more confidence.

It is more difficult, however, to be confident about the wine. Even in the heart of a wine zone there may be no more on offer than a carafe of house wine; it might be divine or it might be dreary. If in doubt, the red is a safer bet.

Top *Onions, grown widely, are as important for flavouring as garlic.* Above *Fresh* cozze *mussels are plentiful along the coast as are many varieties of fish and seafood.*

The only other possible difficulty might be the lack of a written menu. Even in good restaurants the dishes may simply be recited at break-neck speed. Just gesticulate for a slower repetition or if the waiter or owner offers to choose for you, let him. He will be delighted. In any event, eating out is generally far less formal than in the UK. There is no dress code either. And children are expected to join in the feast.

The good restaurants and *trattorie* are always busy and most close annually for a few weeks for holidays or repairs – at unpredictable periods. So it is always worth booking first.

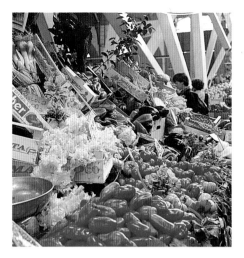

Above *Florence's bustling San Lorenzo market.*
Bottom Pappardelle, *flat, broad noodles, are one of the most typical pasta shapes in Tuscany.*

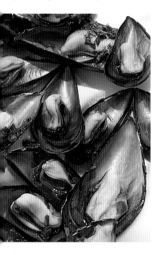

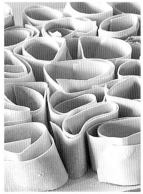

THE TUSCAN MEAL

A meal typically begins with antipasti of *crostini*, small rounds of bread covered with minced chicken liver, *milza* (spleen) or other topping; or *bruschetta*, toasted Tuscan bread rubbed with garlic, drenched in olive oil and possibly topped with tomatoes or black cabbage. There is usually also a plate of *salumi* – salami and cured meats.

The first course, the *primo*, is often pasta, usually *pappardelle*, flat, broad strips; *pinci* or *pici*, thick, hand-rolled spaghetti (a speciality of Montepulciano and Montalcino) or ravioli, filled with meat or spinach and ricotta. Sauces are commonly meat based; *lepre* (hare), *coniglio* (rabbit) and *anatra* (duck) are the classics while *funghi* (mushroom) sauces and *tartufi* (truffles) are popular in season. Alternatively, there are thick soups that rank as *cucina povera*, 'poor folk's food'. *Ribollita* is a slow-cooked vegetable mass, classically based on cabbage, with bread for bulk and thickening; *zuppa di pane* is literally bread soup but given a lift, usually by tomatoes; *panzanella* is a cold summer version, more like salad than soup. More substantial are pulse-based soups; combinations of *fagioli* (white kidney beans), *lenticchie* (lentils), *ceci* (chick peas) and *farro* (a delicious barley-like grain) dominate.

On to the *secondo*, the main course. The flagship is *La Fiorentina*, a giant grilled T-bone steak from the local *Chianina* cattle (or *Maremmana* cattle in the south). *Agnello* (lamb) and *pollo* (chicken) are popular, as are *coniglio*, *lepre*, or *salsiccia* (meaty sausage). Many places will serve three or four 'taster' portions together. A great speciality is *trippa* (tripe), usually cooked with tomatoes. *Fagioli* are also commonly used as an alternative to seasonal vegetables or an (often unexciting) salad.

Tuscans are rightfully proud of their cheeses. *Pecorino*, from ewe's milk, can either be *fresco* (young and soft) or *stagionato* (matured, firm and stronger). *Caprino* is goat's milk cheese.

For *dolce* or dessert, most typical are *cantucci* (almond biscuits), best dunked in a glass of Vin Santo. Other desserts are often bought-in. Traditional Tuscan desserts are less rich than these: cake-like and dryish, often made with chestnut flour – always worth indulging in if *fatti a casa* (home-made).

FOOD SHOPPING

Italians still prefer to shop daily at small specialist shops, so few supermarkets offer the range and quality of the UK chains. However every village has its butcher, cheese shop and *salumeria* (for cured meats, salami, prosciutto etc) and fresh bread is widely available, as are fruit and vegetables. Most towns also have daily (morning) markets. Just remember that shops close in the early afternoon while shopkeepers lunch and have a snooze.

Olive oil

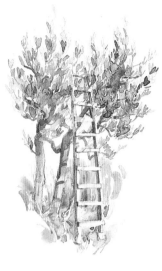

Although Tuscany is usually regarded primarily as a wine region and its olive oil as merely a complementary crop, the abundance of olive trees and the spasmodic nature of vineyards (except in Chianti Classico, Montepulciano and Montalcino) suggest that it should be the reverse. Olive oil is as central to Tuscany's agricultural economy as it is to its diet.

The glories of Tuscan extra virgin olive oil came to notice swiftly in 1985. In January of that year, a cold snap of rare force hit Italy. Temperatures were so low that many olive trees were killed off and most were reduced to bare stumps. Naturally, the price of oil soared. Yet every cloud ... and the resultant publicity stimulated northern Europe's fascination with fine olive oil. Now healthy new growth sits on thick, old trunks while many producers have taken the opportunity of replacing old trees with newer, better varieties and plantation systems. The interest in fine oil has not diminished and though demand keeps prices for the best extra virgin buoyant, they are no longer exorbitant.

Making fine olive oil is expensive and labour-intensive. There is as much debate concerning the best varieties,

Below *Olive oil, flavoured with bay, chilli and fennel. It is best, though, enjoyed 'straight' for its fruity, sometimes spicy, tones.*

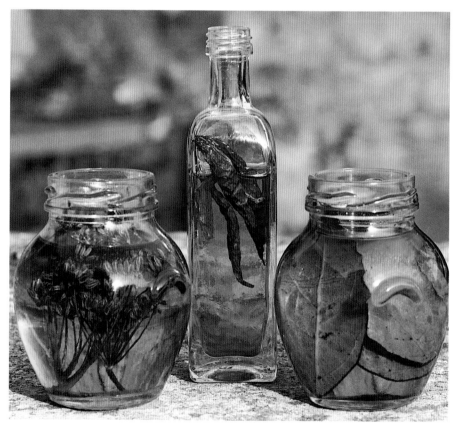

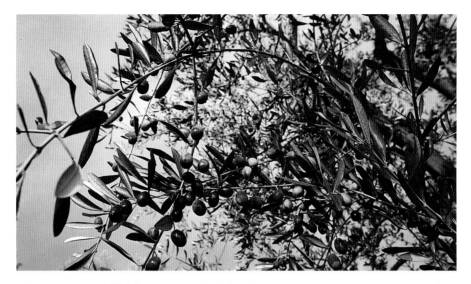

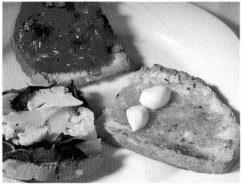

Top *Olive trees are never far from sight in Tuscany and in some areas, such as around Lucca, the Central Hills and the Maremma, they dominate the landscape.*
Above *Top-quality olive oil can lift even the most mundane dishes, such as these* bruschette.

pruning systems and plantation densities as there is for vines. Generally olive trees need much more separation – three metres on average, and up to ten. Olives should be stripped by hand. Nets may be hung underneath to catch them, but not too low as the olives will be bruised as they land. Bruising increases acidity, thus reducing the oil's quality: once acidity exceeds one percent, the oil can no longer be 'extra' and becomes simply 'virgin'. Most really good oil has barely a third of one per cent.

The olive harvest can stretch over several months, starting just after the grape harvest. The earlier-picked olives are still green, the later-picked ones more purple, and the taste of the oil changes from zippy and peppery, to sweeter and more fruity.

In a traditional *frantoio* (oil processing plant) the olives are washed and put in an open granite grinder where they are slowly crushed. The pulp is spread on round mats called *fiscoli* which are then stacked on the press. Downward pressure is applied and the olive liquid separates from the solids. At this point the liquid is a mixture of oil and water. Most producers use a centrifuge to separate the two but a few prefer to leave the liquid to settle and skim off the oil as it rises. The best oil is then ready, unfiltered, but many producers lightly filter the oil for extra clarity.

Large estates may have their own *frantoio* but most growers take their olives to one located nearby. Some have mechanized the process and are convinced that quality does not suffer. Oils from Chianti Classico have regulations similar to those for wine and the rest of Tuscany is gradually following.

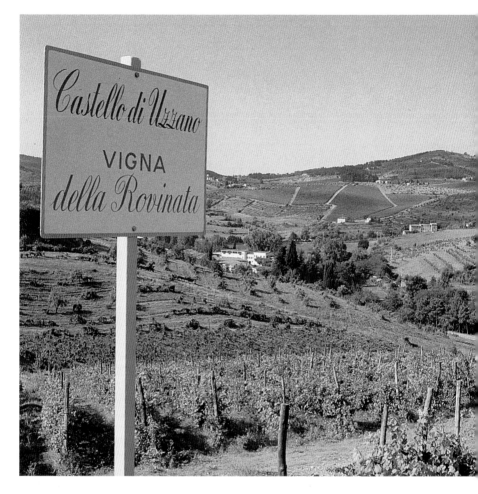

How to use this guide

Above *Some vineyards, such as this one in Chianti Classico, are sign-posted. Many are not, but this guide tells you exactly what lies where.*

Anyone touring Tuscany equipped simply with a map could not help but find vineyards along the way, plus olive groves, charming medieval villages and perhaps the odd wine estate shop. The route would be beautiful – in Tuscany, you can hardly fail to find terrific scenery, and you would come home inspired. But you would not, unless you were very lucky, see the finest tracts of vineyard; understand why vines grow where they do; know if the wine you bought was as good as the district could produce, or was typical or unusual. The aim of this book is to help you achieve these aims. It is for anyone who, at least sometime during their trip, would like to see the vines and wine estates, taste the wines, meet producers and learn a little about their craft without ignoring Tuscany's other splendours.

The book takes the form of a series of shortish routes, trips which take anything from half an hour to the best part

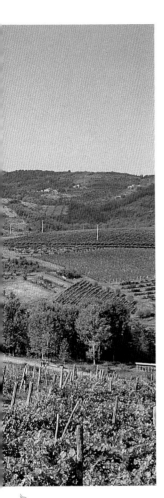

of a day. Each route leads through a particular part of Tuscany's wine lands. If wine is an adjunct to a more general tour, pick any route coinciding with wherever you are. Alternatively, let one route lead to the next.

The guide itself begins and ends in Florence, but the tour can be joined at any point. Those driving up from Rome could start at Grosseto (p99), those flying to Pisa could start there (p122). Those heading along the Autostrada del Sole could pick up the route at Arezzo (p78). You can skip bits along the way or plunge in even deeper: the itineraries take all needs into account. The approximate timings given are based on the assumption that within wine areas you will move at a fairly leisurely pace, stopping from time to time; while between the wine areas you will drive reasonably fast.

Convenient stopping-off places are pointed out too, together with suggestions for places to stay.

WINE PRODUCERS

Thumb-nail sketches of local producers form an important part of the book. Those that are included have been chosen mainly for the quality of their wines but also for their location along the routes. So, if an estate is not included it does not necessarily mean its wines are not up to scratch it could simply be that it is situated too far off the beaten track.

MAPS

Wine maps (see below) illustrating main routes are included.

RESTAURANTS

There are suggestions for eating out, from the smartest restaurant to the simplest *trattoria,* many with tables outdoors in summer and most featuring good wines, be they the more esoteric bottles or simply unusually good house wine. The better shops are listed too, for those self-catering, planning picnics, or wanting something intriguing to take home, and naturally the *enoteche,* places to buy and taste wine, are highlighted.

HOTELS

For wine-lovers, *agriturismo* apartments are often the best place to stay when in Tuscany (see p13). A short selection of characterful hotels has also been included in the listings.

PLACES OF INTEREST

Tuscany is steeped in history and cultural interest and we pinpoint the most important, together with any special events with a wine or food interest.

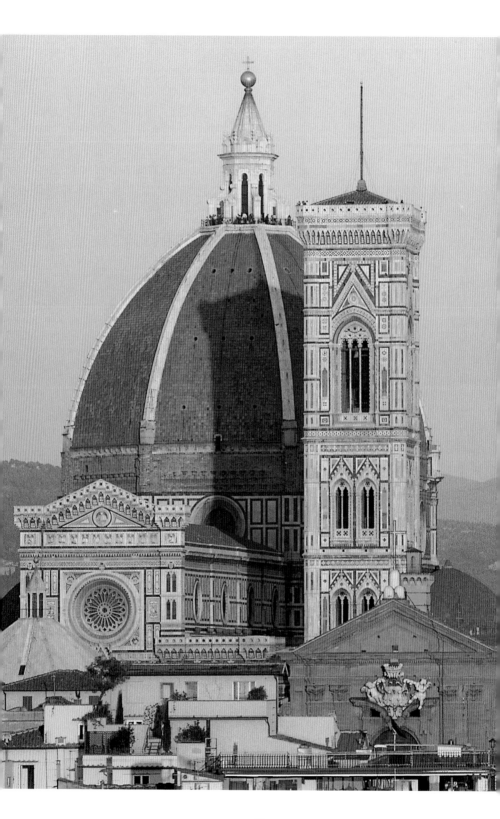

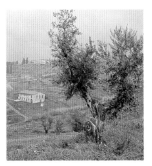

Florence

For a city with one of the world's most important wine districts on its doorstep, Florence is reticent about its wine links. There is not an *enoteca* on every corner, nor are there shops full of wine memorabilia. Perhaps Florence has so many other attractions it can afford to ignore those outside its gates. Admittedly, wine is not ignored completely, but if you want to spend a few days among the splendours of this city without thinking about wine too much, it can easily be done.

And what splendours they are. The alluring *Duomo* (cathedral), visible for miles around but surprisingly squat close to, is the focal point. The Palazzo Vecchio, appearing almost like a cardboard cut-out, overlooks the elegant Piazza della Signoria, which is a good spot to watch the world go by over an (expensive) drink, as is the more bustling Piazza della Repubblica. The Ponte Vecchio, lined with jewellery shops, and its pavements crowded with street traders, is the Arno's most atmospheric bridge, but others (and there are several) give better views of the city and of the river itself. Depending on the time of year, the Arno can be a languorous trickle or a surging torrent. Other 'musts' are the Franciscan church of Santa Croce and its severe, rectangular piazza; the Medici Palace and the church of San Lorenzo; the church of Santa Maria Novella near the station and the convent of San Marco, which is now a museum.

Museum opening times have now been extended from the pitiful few they once were. Even so, queues for the Uffizi gallery are often long. No wonder, considering its unrivalled collection of Renaissance art. The Pitti Palace houses a further impressive collection, and a museum. For relief, the Boboli Gardens are beautifully laid out and offer cool strolls and splendid views. Even better views are seen from Piazzale Michelangelo, just beyond the city walls. The walls them-

The ubiquitous olive tree (top) *is as much a powerful symbol of rural Tuscany as the magnificent*

Renaissance Duomo (left) *which dominates the Florence skyline, is of its capital city.*

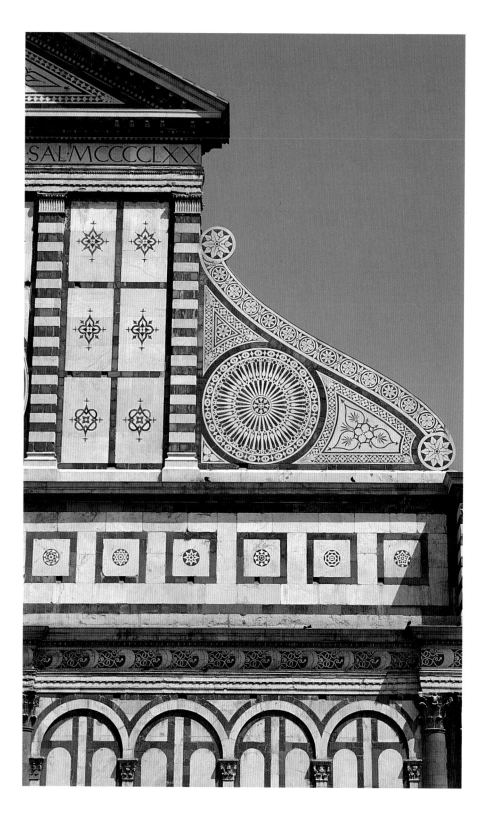

selves are captivating, still standing in spite of the incessant traffic, as is the huge old fortress, the Fortezza da Basso.

And so it goes until your feet are sore and your head is overwhelmed – and you still will have done little more than brush the surface of this stunning city.

The quieter, narrow, cobbled streets of Florence are relaxing to stroll through and reveal a city where aesthetic appeal is found worked into delightful detail on roofs, cornices and even lamp posts. Alternatively, try window-shopping in and around the smart streets around the Via dei Calzaiuoli and Via Tornabuoni – unless your credit card feels strong enough for a purchase.

Eventually, however, you will need to sit down and feed the body as well as the soul, and it is at this point that your thoughts may return to wine.

WINE IN FLORENCE
Most restaurants and *trattorie* will have a decent selection of Chianti Classico and other local wines so drinking well with meals is not a problem. *Vinerie* are the city's old wine bars. A *vineria* used not to be chic, being more the haunt of elderly men swigging down small glasses filled to the rim. Now they attract all ages, usually serve wine properly, but are still fun and bursting with character. Good ones are in Via de'Neri, Via Sant'Antonio and Via dell'Ariento (near the market), Via degli Alfani (by the University), Gonnelli (by the station), Via de Castellani (near Palazzo Vecchio), Piazza dell'Olio, and by the San Pierino Arch.

If you want to buy wine, move away from the central touristy areas towards the areas where Florentines live, around the Via de'Serragli in Oltrarno (the southern side of the Arno), for example, which boasts a wine equipment shop, or north of Piazza San Marco. Traditional wine shops are called *fiaschetterie*, after the flasks (*fiaschi*) in which Chianti was once sold. Some look rather down-at-heel but can be Aladdin's caves inside. There are also a number of smarter, more modern wine shops springing up, usually called *Enoteche* (see p10), although at least one, in Via de'Serragli, calls itself a *Bottiglioteca*. Clearly Florentines, in naming as much as everything else, are very style-conscious.

Florence also has several excellent book shops with a range of books (in Italian) on all aspects of wine.

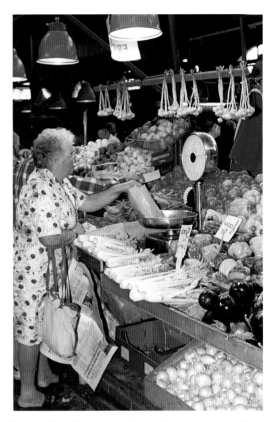

Above *Fresh fruit and vegetables at the main San Lorenzo market.*
Left *Santa Maria Novella's splendid façade.*

EATING OUT

Caffè Concerto
Lungarno C. Colombo, 7
Tel: 055 677377; cl. Sun
Pretty restaurant with great views, a vast wine list, prime ingredients and fine, inventive dishes. Reasonably priced.

La Casalinga
Via dei Michelozzi, 9r
Tel: 055 218624; cl. Sun
Good value, centrally located trattoria, popular with local Florentines. Classic Tuscan fare. Drink house.

Cibreo (1)
Via de' Macci, 118r
Tel: 055 2341100; cl. Sun, Mon
One of Florence's long-standing top spots. Memorable dishes and inspired use of ingredients. Wine list to match.

Cibreo (2)
Piazza Ghiberti, 35
Round the corner from its famous brother; simpler, cheaper. Popular but no bookings: turn up and wait. Cash only.

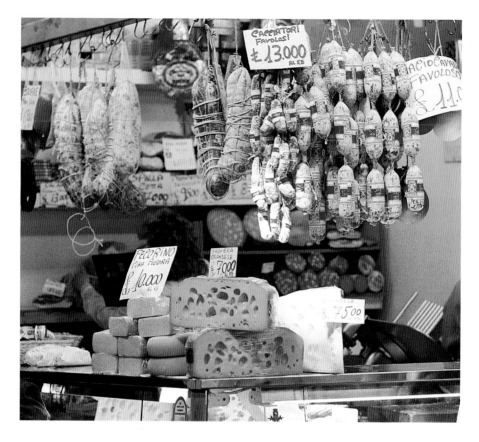

Above *The central San Lorenzo market has plentiful supplies of* salumi *and cheeses.*

Da Sergio
Piazza San Lorenzo, 8r
Tel: 055 281941; cl. Sun
Classic dishes, few choices, huge portions. Drink house. Cheap. Cash only.

Don Chisciotte
Via C. Ridolfi, 4r
Tel: 055 475430; cl. Sun
Go for the ace fish and a break from Tuscan norms. Good wine list. Value.

Enoteca Pinchiorri
Via Ghibellina, 87
Tel: 055 242777; cl. Wed lunch, Sun, Mon
Furiously expensive and very smart; one of Italy's top five restaurants. The wine list astounds. Must book.

Orologio
Piazza Ferrucci, 1
Tel: 055 6811729; cl. Sat eve, Sun
Long-standing, inexpensive, typical trattoria, frequented by Florentines.

Ottorino
Via delle Oche, 18/22r
Tel: 055 218747; cl. Sun

FOOD IN FLORENCE

To find food shops in Florence go a few hundred metres out of the centre, where they cluster in abundance. There are *alimentari* (general grocers) and *pizzicherie* (delicatessen), the Florentine equivalent of the more usual word *gastronomie*.

Florentines also shop at the central market, Mercato San Lorenzo, and the smaller Mercato Sant'Ambrogio (Piazza Ghiberti). The former, enclosed in a fine ironwork building and open every morning (except Sundays) is on two floors and offers a huge selection of fruit and vegetables (including organically grown varieties) upstairs. Downstairs bread, meat, poultry, fish, *salumi*, cheese, eggs, nuts and pulses, even confectionery, are available. There's also an in-house self-service *trattoria*, Da Nerbone, which serves simple, nourishing but remarkably good quick meals. The smaller Sant'Ambrogio market is useful mainly for its greengrocery, concentrating on produce from small growers from the surrounding countryside.

There is no shortage of places to eat in the centre. If anything the abundance is overwhelming, with scarcely a street food-free, from ice-cream and snack spots to the most sophisticated of restaurants. Try Il Pizzaiuolo in Via de' Macci. It will be worth it, despite the queues. For a good

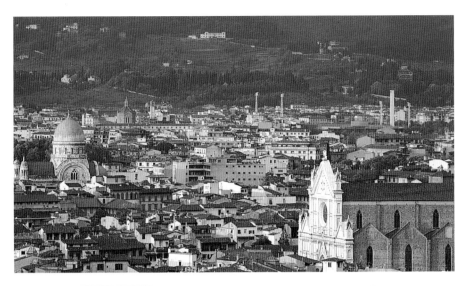

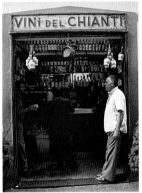

Above *View of Florence with the Santa Croce chapel in the foreground.*
Left *A traditional Florentine vineria.*

Long-standing, friendly restaurant, serving impeccable, simple Tuscan classics. Shortish but fair wine list.
Pane e Vino
Via San Niccolò, 70a/r
Tel: 055 2476956; eves only, cl. Sun
Great spot. Tasty, inventive food; calm, friendly atmosphere. Cheese board a speciality. Very good value.
La Vecchia Cucina
Viale E. De Amicis, 1r
Tel: 055 660143; cl. Sat lunch, Sun
Top quality ingredients; light, flavoursome dishes. Tasting menu. Fine wine list. Good value. Welcoming.

ENOTECHE

Le Volpi e l'Uva
Piazza dei Rossi, 1r
Tel: 055 239813 2; cl. Sun, late eves
Fun place with wines from lesser-known producers by glass and bottle.
Fuori Porta
Via Monte alle Croci, 10
Tel: 055 2342483; cl. Sun
The place to go. Hundreds of wines, good snacks, great atmosphere.
Cantinetta dei Verrazzano
Via dei Tavolini, 18-20
Tel: 055 268590; cl. Sun, late eves
Relaxing wine bar. Wines from Castello di Verrazzano. Abundant snacks.
Mario
Via della Rosina, 2r
Tel: 055 218550; lunch only, cl Sun
Part tratt, part wine bar. Join the locals at a long bench.
Vini Vecchi Sapori
Via dei Mazaggini, 3r
Tel: 055 293045; cl. Mon
New, informal, wines by glass and bottle, beers too. Snacks or full meals.

sandwich on the hoof, stop at the stand of Palmino Pinzauti, Piazza de'Cimatori. In the same square, Birreria Centrale serves good Bavarian beer and a nibble or two to help it down.

For the really brave, though, there's the true Florentine snack food: *lampredutto*, veal tripe, served as a sandwich in crispy bread. Good outlets are in Via dell'Ariento, Piazza de'Cimatori, Via Gioberti, Via de'Macci and Piazzale di Porta Romana. Try! You'll find it nowhere else in Italy.

It would be unthinkable to visit Florence without indulging in an ice cream. If you want to experience the best home-made flavours and textures go to Vivoli, Via Isole delle Stinche.

DRIVING IN FLORENCE

The rules on access to the city for motorists are unusually complicated. Cars may or may not be allowed in depending on the day of the week, whether or not the car has a cat-alytic converter and where it comes from. If you can't understand the signs, ask, or you risk a painful fine.

East of Florence

Heading eastward from Florence towards Pontassieve can prove to be a rather slow and relatively uninteresting stretch of road. The scenery is not Tuscany's finest and the traffic can be heavy. It is best to keep south of the river and make for Bagno a Ripoli, shortly after which a section of dual carriageway speeds up the journey.

The functional small town of Pontassieve itself marks the confluence of the River Arno as it bends west towards Florence and its tributary, the south-flowing Sieve. Traffic once poured in from both these river valleys and from the Casentino to the east (see below). The inevitable snarl-ups gave full vent to Italian motoring expressionism and the long-awaited by-pass has done much to lower blood pressure.

The Arno rises not far from Pontassieve but takes a magnificent horseshoe course, first southward through Poppi and Bibbiena, a beautiful sweep known as the Casentino. It is more reminiscent of Switzerland than Italy and is dotted with castles and Romanesque abbeys. Neither wine nor olives are produced here.

The river turns on its tail just above Arezzo and flows back to the northwest before meeting the Sieve. In this second stretch, the Val d'Arno Superiore (the Upper Arno Valley), olive cultivation is much in evidence as are flourishing vines. The more southern areas are part of Chianti Colli Aretini, while the middle ranges fall inside Chianti Colli Fiorentini.

Only the part closest to the Sieve is within Chianti

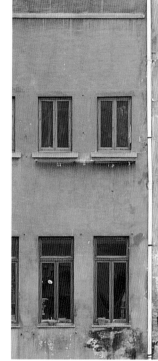

Above *The faded grandeur of buildings along the Arno (Lungarno) in Florence. From the city, the wine zone of Chianti Rufina can be reached in half an hour.*

Left *Tuscans expend great efforts with flowers to make the outside of their homes colourful and welcoming.*

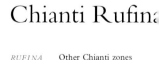

Bologna

Chianti Rufina

RUFINA	Other Chianti zones
POMINO	Other DOC
CASALINO	Important cellars
☐	Vineyards
☐	Areas not legally Chianti
☐	Woods
═250═	Contour interval 50 metres
▬	Wine route

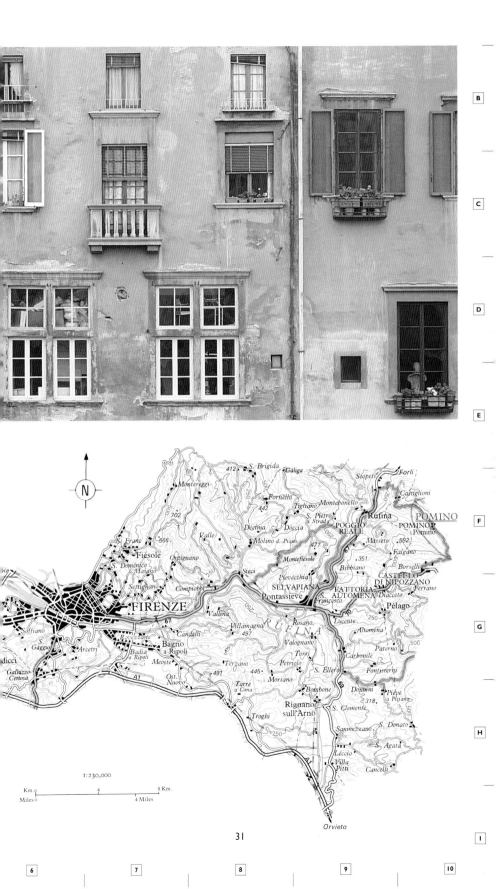

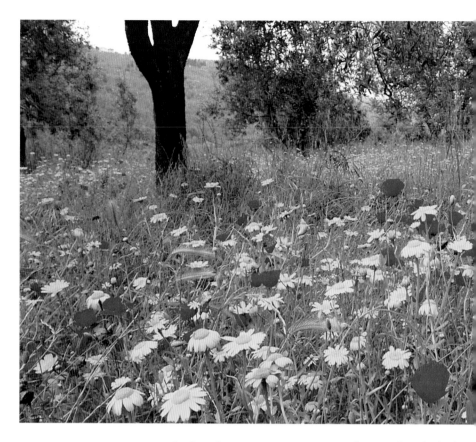

CHIANTI RUFINA

RECOMMENDED PRODUCERS

Fattoria Selvapiana
Pontassieve
Tel: 055 8369848; E, G, F
Both the classiest and friendliest of
many an estate. Now run by the
more than capable Federico Masetti
who has stamped additional character
onto wines which never lacked style.
Chianti Rufina is complex, elegant,
piercing and long-lasting; cru
Bucerchiale defines the better years;
Vin Santo; Borro Lastricato, fresh
white, from Pinot Bianco, Pinot Grigio.
Fabulous olive oil.

Marchesi di Frescobaldi
Pontassieve
Tel: 055 27141; E, G
Large company, run by the
Frescobaldi family. Over six centuries
of winemaking experience, 800ha of
vineyard across several estates and
numerous wines. From 900-year old
Castello di Nipozzano, the major
estate, Chianti Rufina Riserva crus
Nipozzano and highly rated
Montesodi, super-tuscan Mormoreto;

Rufina, forming a compact zone of extraordinarily high
potential, which is gradually becoming better known and
better exploited.

CHIANTI RUFINA

Chianti Rufina straddles the Sieve Valley from Pontassieve
upriver to Dicomano. The basic blend of grapes and
production criteria are essentially the same as they are in
Chianti Classico, but the Rufina wine is somewhat
firmer, more acidic, more structured and therefore longer-
living than the majority of Classico. This is due partly to
the sandy calcareous soils and partly to the narrowness of
the Sieve Valley, which traps heat by day and loses then it
by night.

Despite this innate pedigree, only two estates have a
truly reliable track record: Marchesi di Frescobaldi, with
more than 500ha of vine and numerous estates which
dominate the scenery, and Fattoria Selvapiana, which has
the more finely tuned wines. Other estates are slowly
emerging. Yet some vines look like they are run-down and
uncared for.

There is also a certain amount of confusion between the
area Rufina (accented on the first syllable) and the big

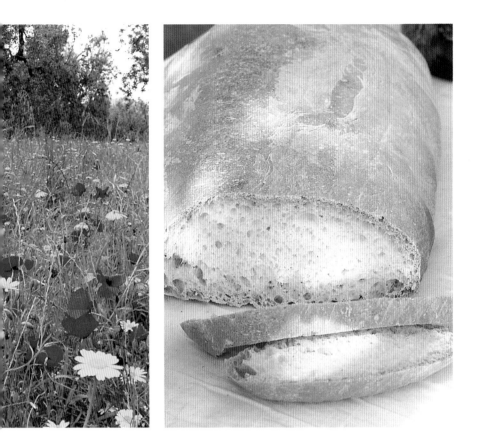

Chianti Classico house Ruffino, which doesn't help. However, the Rufina Consorzio is doing much to develop the zone's profile and encourages member estates to welcome visitors.

A short loop from Pontassieve gives good sightings of the estates on the right bank of the Sieve. Cross the river at Pontassieve and follow it to Montebonello, then take a turning inland to San Pietro a Strada and Monterifrassine, joining the main road from Florence to Pontassieve just below Sieci.

The first estate you see is Fattoria di Basciano, on the right, with its renovated medieval tower; then (left) you see Villa di Vetrice with a 12th-century tower. After Monterifrassine, Fattoria di Lavacchio appears, followed by Tenuta di Bossi, a 15th-century villa, both of which are on the left. The tall medieval tower, visible from time to time in the middle distance as the road curves, is the Torre di Arcone.

The heart of Rufina and its two most important estates lie south of the Sieve. From Pontassieve head south along the Upper Arno, following the railway. Shortly, to see Frescobaldi's Castello di Nipozzano and explore the Casentino, take a turning left towards Vallombrosa

Above left Spring in Tuscany brings a riot of flowers.
Above Tuscan bread, firm but unsalted, is a staple.

from Remole, Chianti Rufina Remole; from Tenuta di Pomino, Pomino red and white plus oaked white Pomino II Benefizio; plus others. Also owns Castelgiocondo estate in Montalcino.

Tenuta Bossi Marchese Gondi
Pontassieve
Tel: 055 8317830; fax:: 8364008; E, F.
Up and coming estate. Chianti Rufinas San Giuliano, Marchese Gondi (Riserva) and Villa Bossi (barriqued) lead range. Notable Mazzaferrata (Cabernet) and Vin Santo. Vineyards adjacent. Visits only afternoons or Sat. morning. Book with estate several months prior.

Fattoria di Petrognano
Pomino
Tel: 055 8318812; fax:: 8364008
Wine, housed in ancient underground cellars is made by Selvapiana. Apartments scattered over an expanse of olive grove and vineyard in Pomino. Tennis courts. Small hotel

and restaurant serving simple, traditional Tuscan meals. Closed Oct-Easter.

Fattoria di Basciano
Rufina
Tel: 055 8397034; fax: 8399250; E
Softish Chianti Rufina; firmer Riserva. I Pini and Il Corto blend Sangiovese and Cabernet in different proportions to good effect. Also Vin Santo and others. Must book rooms with estate 3-4 months prior.

Villa di Vetrice
Rufina
Tel: 055 8397008
Friendly estate. Abundantly drinkable, good value Chianti Rufina, approachable Vin Santo. Must book.

HOTELS

Both Pontassieve and Rufina have hotels, the **Moderno** and **La**

Below and right *Fattoria Selvapiana's cellars and vineyards are more elegant than their sales points. They also produce some of Tuscany's finest olive oil.*

and Passo della Consuma. Otherwise keep going for a circuit through the essence of Rufina, taking a couple of leisurely hours.

The area is liberally dotted with some medieval houses. The more important habitations were necessarily fortressed. But the *case coloniche*, simple workers' houses, have a satisfying solidity and an elegance of design that is difficult to match. The first to appear on the right are absolutely typical.

The first vineyards, on the left, are leased by the estate Castello di Trebbio (a 13th-century castle situated at northerly Santa Brigida, outside Rufina). Some less tended vineyards follow before the imposing Castello Volognano emerges across the river. On a clear day the steep slopes of Gaiole in Chianti Classico (see p.62) are visible in front.

At Sant'Ellero, head left for Vallombrosa. The tower situated on the left marks a small former monastery. Within a matter of seconds, the road begins to rise and woodland replaces vines. This area, spanning the ridge between the upper Val d'Arno and Vallombrosa,

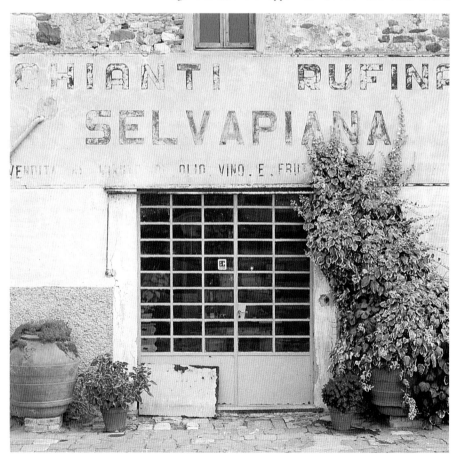

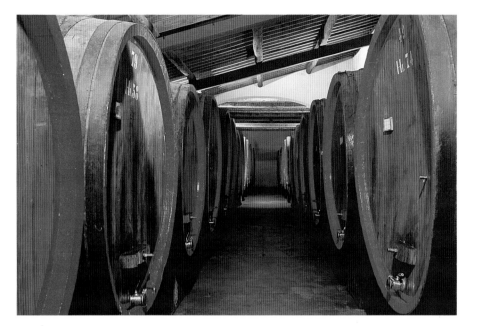

is outside Chianti Rufina and is called the Pratomagno. Again, there is a mixture of medieval and Renaissance architecture.

Here you may add in an optional (long) extension to the tour by taking the side-road to the right, to Pieve a Pitiana, one of a number of simple but powerful Romanesque churches found along the Upper Arno, and the 'Road of the Seven Bridges', so-called because it hops over each of the Upper Arno's tributaries.

Otherwise, have a peek at the Villa Pitiana (left) before continuing up to Tosi with its views over Rufina and its amphitheatre of olive and vine. Craft workers in wooden furniture abound in the village.

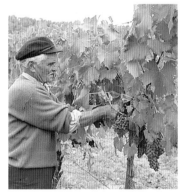

Next head for Saltino. Reaching the Pian di Melusa, you are surrounded by thick pine forest which looks distinctly more Tyrolean than Tuscan. The forest was owned by monks until 1860, and then it was taken over by the Forestry Commission, but it was partially restored to its original owners in 1949. A combination of fir, pine, and beech ensures a stunning array of colour throughout the year.

At 1,000m the road bends sharply, and out of nowhere appears the monastery of Vallombrosa. The touring route is then downhill through forest that is interspersed with gushing waterfalls until Consuma, where the countryside opens right out and vine and olive vistas return. Here Chianti Rufina temporarily becomes Pomino.

Speranza respectively. But since both towns are rather dreary, stay elsewhere if possible.

Villa Pitiana
Donnini
Tel: 055 860259; fax: 055 860326
A magnificent complex of opulent hotel (3*), agritourism apartments and restaurant attached to the cloisters of an ancient Vallombrosano monastery. Fabulous views over the Arno to Chianti Classico. Swimming pool. Food traditional but refined – probably the best in the Rufina area. Hotel open Apr-Oct incl. Restaurant open weekends only during winter months. Not overly expensive; excellent value.

AGRITURISMO

The following estates have *agriturismo* apartments. See also under Recommended Producers.

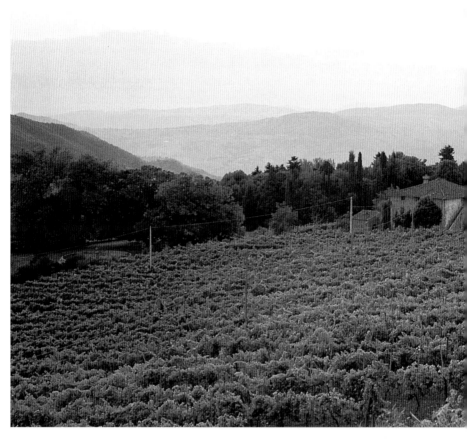

Fattoria di Petrognano
Tel: 055 8318812
Wine, housed in ancient underground cellars, is made by Selvapiana. Own trattoria. Closed October to Easter.
Fattoria di Basciano
Montebonello Tel: 055 8397034
Fattoria il Frantoio
Dicomano Tel: 055 8397886
Az Agr Capiteto
Acone Tel: 055 8361600
With swimming pool
Soggiorno al Lago
Vicchio Tel: 055 8448638
With swimming, horse riding, mountain biking and other activities.

ENOTECA

Politi
Rufina

EATING OUT

La Casellina
Pontassieve, Via Colognolese, 28
Tel: 055 8397580; cl. Tue in winter, Mon
Trattoria on the Montebonello road. True Tuscan fare without clichés. Good range of Tuscan and Italian

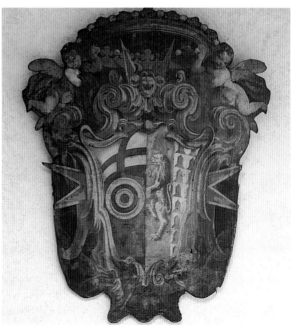

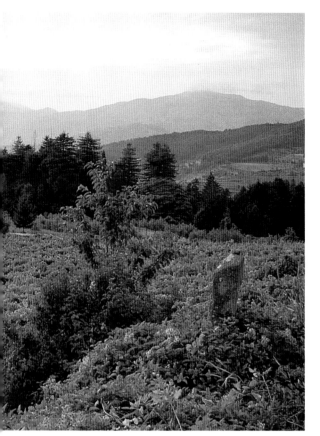

Main picture *Overlooking Pomino and Chianti Rufina. Most of the Pomino valley belongs to the Frescobaldi, which has vineyards across several estates.*
Below left *Frescobaldi's coat-of-arms. The family has over six centuries of winemaking experience.*

POMINO

Pomino abuts and slightly overlaps Chianti Rufina. The zone centres on Pomino village and is bordered by the Rufina stream, which runs into the Sieve at Rufina itself. It is one of Italy's smallest DOC zones and was also one of the first to be denominated, in 1716.

In the mid-19th century Marchese Vittorio degli Albizi planted French grape varieties here, and the tradition remains. Whites are mainly from Pinot Bianco and Chardonnay; reds are from Sangiovese but mixed with Cabernet, Merlot and sometimes Pinot Nero. For long, Frescobaldi ruled unchallenged. Now Fattoria Selvapiana has entered the fray, having rented the vineyards of Fattoria di Petrognano and the wines are causing quite a stir.

At Consuma turn left, towards Pontassieve, following the zone's boundary. The smart Renaissance house on the right is Spedaletto, one of Frescobaldi's many villas. After a brief wooded stretch you are rewarded by a panoramic view to the right over the whole Pomino valley. Shortly the Romanesque church of Tosina appears on the left, a good spot for sweeping views,

wines. Seats outdoors. Very good value.

Vicolo del Contento
Castelfranco di Sopra (Pratomagno)
Tel: 055 9149277; cl. Mon, Tue
Good quality restaurant in 15th century village along the Upper Arno unusually built to a grid system. Smart, modern. Well flavoured, enticing food. Fish a speciality. Tasting menu. Well chosen wines, mainly local. Seats outside. Fair value.

La Tana degli Orsi
Pratovecchio, Via Roma, 1
Tel: 0575 583377; eves only, cl. Wed.
Relaxed restaurant. Fine, inventive dishes from classic Tuscan ingredients. Long wine list, several by glass. Seats outside. Very good value.

Accaniti
Pratovecchio, Via Fiorentina, 14
Tel: 0575 583345; cl. Tue
Simple, easy-going place, simple food but carefully prepared and well cooked. Decent wine list. Very good value.

Centanni
Bagno a Ripoli, Via dei Centanni, 8
Tel: 055 630122
Long-standing, well run restaurant. Strictly traditional Tuscan dishes. Carefully sourced wines. Seats outside. Good views. Good value.

PLACES OF INTEREST

Villa Poggio Reale/Chianti Rufina Museum
Rufina. *Tel: 055 8396111*
Carefully restored 16th century villa said to be designed by Michelangelo but probably the work of his followers. Houses the Chianti Rufina Museum of Vine and Wine. Viewing by appointment. Contact the Ufficio Cultura of the Comune di Rufina.

Monastery of Vallombrosa
The Vallombrosano was an order of monks derived from the Benedictine. This commanding building hugged by pine forests is high in the Pratomagno. Remains of the kitchen

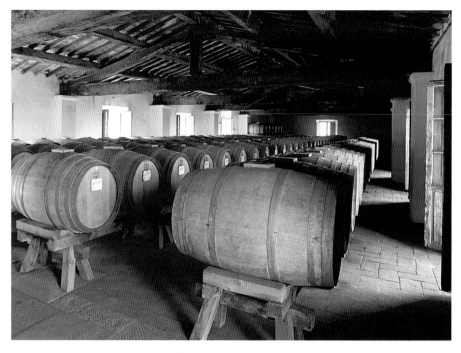

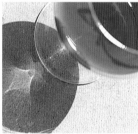

Top *Casks of Vin Santo mature in Frescobaldi's cellars in Pomino.*
Right *Vineyards surround the villa of Selvapiana, producer of complex and elegant Chianti Rufina.*

garden and trout lake lead to the crested entrance. The church is always open. The abbey can be seen by guided tours at 10.30am Tuesdays and Fridays between June and September.

FOOD SHOPPING

Cooperative Il Forteto
To the right, heading up the Sieve between Dicomano and Vicchio. Youngsters recovering from drug-related and other problems produce and sell superb sheep and goats' cheeses (the *Pecorino* is wonderful),

focused on the Rufina stream snaking into the Sieve valley.

Just before Pomino village, to the left, you'll see a long, low house with Vin Santo aging in casks behind its windows. This is another Frescobaldi villa, often used for receptions. In Pomino village itself, locate the Pieve di San Bartolomeo. There's a fine Della Robbia inside and outside a rare example of old-fashioned vine culture: vines trained over maple shoots.

A few minutes' down from the village is the Fattoria di Petrognano. Further along on the right, just before the Pomino gives way again to Chianti Rufina, is Pomino's third Romanesque church, the Pieve di Castiglioni.

A few minutes down from the village is the Fattoria di Petrognano. Another few minutes and Pomino gives way to Chianti Rufino once more. Continue to the valley floor. Then turn left and head back through Rufina itself. It is not the prettiest of towns: better to look at the Torre di Arcone punctuating the right bank and the imposing sight of Poggio Reale ahead.

A short distance before Pontassieve there is a terracotta display on the left and an unmarked lane. This is, surprisingly, the driveway to Fattoria Selvapiana, although it is far more imposing further up.

PASSO DEL MURAGLIONE
An optional extra and a really glorious way to spend a morning (to avoid the sun in your eyes) – especially if the

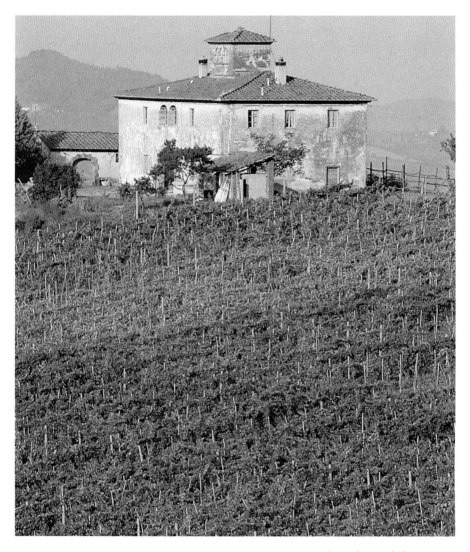

weather is clear – is a visit to the Passo del Muraglione. More than 900m above sea-level, this is the highest peak on the old road over the Apennines, which linked Tuscany and the Adriatic in the days before the advent of motorways.

There is a tall stretch of wall (the *Muraglione*) in the middle of the road, which was reputedly built as a wind-break to stop carriages from being blown off. This is certainly understandable, as the wind up there is ferocious.

Take the road along the Sieve past Rufina to Dicomano then fork to the right. Gradually the road begins to snake upwards and at every third or fourth twist you get increasingly magnificent views of central Tuscany – right across Chianti Classico.

salumeria, honey and other preserves. The produce is also available in Florence's San Lorenzo market.

La Bottega a Rosano
Rosano (Pontassieve)
Various food specialities.

FAIRS

Bacco Artigiano
Rufina: Last week of September, Thursday to Sunday. Exhibition and sale of wines and local crafts.

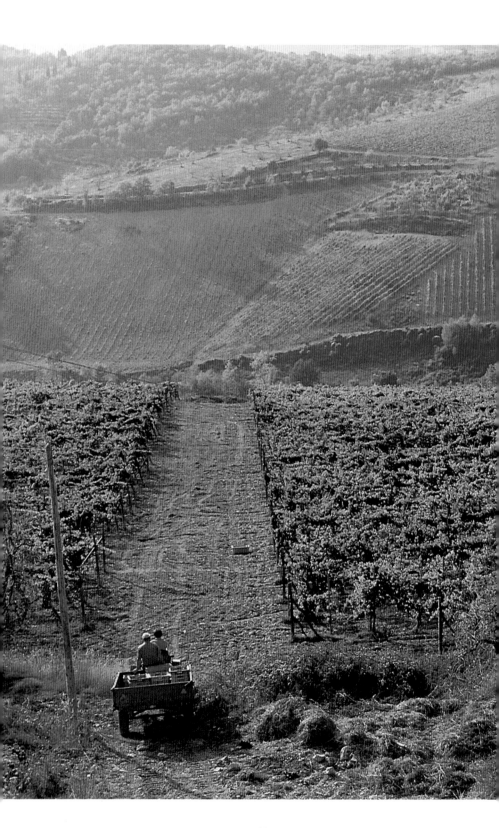

Chianti Classico

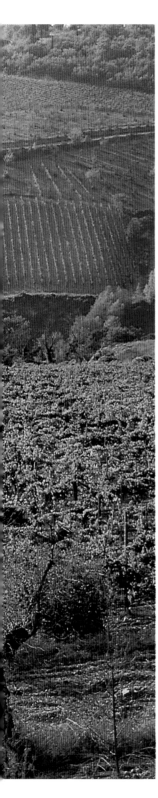

Diverse as Tuscany's scenery is, it is hardly surprising that the entire region has become associated with its most famous part, the land of Chianti Classico. Its 70,000 hectares of hilly land contain some of the most breathtaking views in Europe. There is such variety that it is almost worth getting lost, although efficient signposting makes it difficult to wander aimlessly within the zone. Bumpy tracks apparently heading off to nowhere almost always emerge onto one of the asphalted roads that saunter from village to village.

Chianti Classico can be reached quickly from Florence to the north, Siena to the south and the San Donato exit of the Florence – Siena *super-strada* to the west. For a taster of Chianti Classico's splendours, simply follow the Chiantigiana, the main north–south road. If you're tempted to explore further, do. There's more and better.

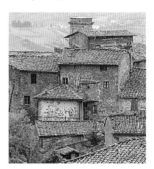

The district has long been called Chianti; the name of the wines followed. The name had such cachet that when wine laws were first promulgated in the 1960s, producers in the surrounding districts grabbed their opportunity to share the benefits. As a result the wine area 'Chianti' is huge, stretching from north of Pistoia to south of Montalcino and from Livorno on the coast to Arezzo inland. The real, historical zone therefore took on the appendix Classico, to indicate the classic heartland. The rest was split into sub-districts, which, with the exception of the small zones of Rufina, Montalbano, and Montespertoli, followed provincial lines: wines from the province of Siena, for example, became Chianti Colli Senesi, those from the province of Pisa, Chianti Colline Pisane and so on. Many would like the name Chianti once more to be restricted to the Classico area only, although this seems unlikely. At least the wine law treats the Classico separately.

Chianti, the wine, is red, its character deriving from the difficult but rewarding Sangiovese grape – difficult because it produces decent wines easily, but requires very skilful handling to make something great; and rewarding because its wines fully reflect the diversity of site from which they come in an infinite variety of complex and subtle variations.

White wine in the area takes very much second place. The local Trebbiano Toscano and Malvasia grape varieties are

Left *Vineyards, olive groves, pine forest and cypresses – typical Chianti countryside.*

Above *Volpaia, with its red rooftops and hill-top position, epitomises a typical Tuscan village.*

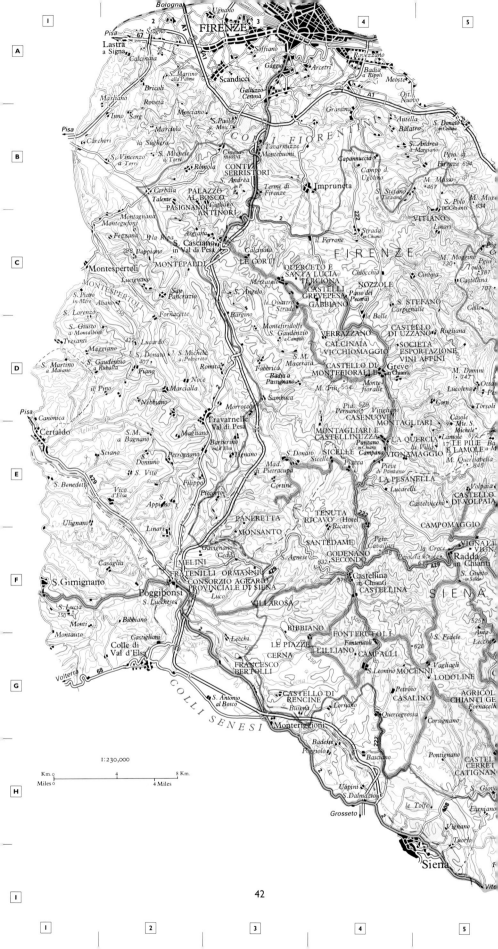

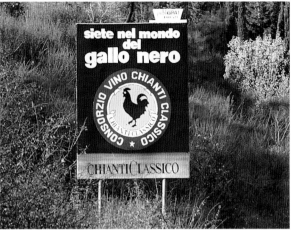

Right *The well known* Gallo Nero *(black cockerel) symbol of the Conzorzio del Marchio Storico-Chianti-Classico, which adorns all its members' bottles.*

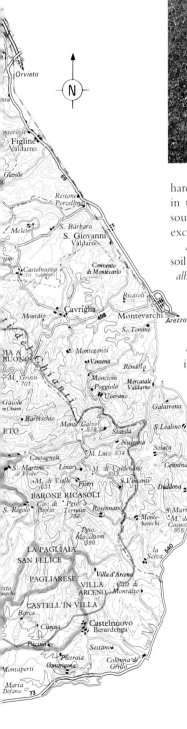

hard pushed to produce wines of personality. They are used in the light, fresh DOC Bianco Val d'Arbia, covering the southern part of the Classico and lands beyond. Their really exciting role, though, is in the flagship Vin Santo.

A geological map of the area reveals a complex pattern of soil outcrops but the vines cluster on the esteemed limestone *alberese,* clay-schist *galestro* or, in the higher areas, sandstone. The highest vineyards top 600m, the lowest are around 250m and, although southwest- or southeast-facing slopes are favoured, vines grow on many aspects.

Starry as Sangiovese is, it is not the sole constituent of Chianti. Small quantities of other grapes are also included. In the mid-19th century the Barone Bettino Ricasoli laid down his formula for the wine, which included the red grape Canaiolo, and the white grapes Trebbiano and Malvasia. The aim, however, was a light, easy-drinking wine, not today's fuller more serious bottles. In 1984, Chianti was up-

Chianti Classico

‒·‒·‒·‒	Provincia boundary
———	Boundary of DOCG Chianti Classico area
RUFINA	Other Chianti zones
POMINO	Other DOC
CASALINO	Important cellars
☐	Vineyards
☐	Areas not legally Chianti
☐	Woods
══250══	Contour interval 50 metres
	Wine route

SAN CASCIANO

RECOMMENDED PRODUCERS

Machiavelli
Tel: 0577 989001
Cellars under the site of Niccolò Macchiavelli's home. Well-structured but rounded wines. Chianti Classico Riserva Fontalle; Ser Niccolò (Cabernet Sauvignon); Il Principe (Pinot Nero). Conti Serristori makes softer, easier wines in same ownership.
Fattoria La Loggia
Tel: 055 8244288; fax: 055 8244283

Below *Shady, winding streets and tiled roofs are typical of towns and villages throughout Tuscany.*

graded to DOCG. The regulation Sangiovese content was increased to 75–90 percent. Now, a new revision will finally allow Chianti Classico to contain unsullied Sangiovese.

Those who do want 100 percent Sangiovese have, until now, either cheated or, more usually, made another wine beside their Chianti Classico. These wines, often a producer's best, have been dubbed 'super-Tuscans', reflecting their quality and erstwhile lack of classification. Other super-Tuscans are more experimental, often blending Sangiovese with Cabernet Sauvignon. (A small proportion of Cabernet is sometimes used in Chianti anyway, to give a riper, fruitier style.) There are non-traditional whites, too, often from Chardonnay or, sometimes, Sauvignon/Sémillon blends. Most of these more innovative wines are aged in *barrique* as is much Chianti Classico, even though *botti* are the traditional ageing vessels. Now, estates are increasingly looking at mid-sized barrels – to great effect.

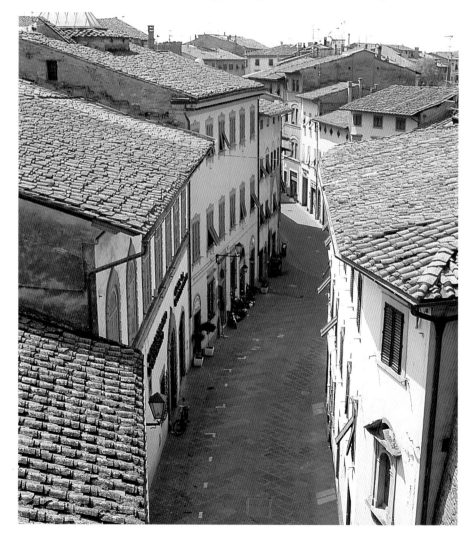

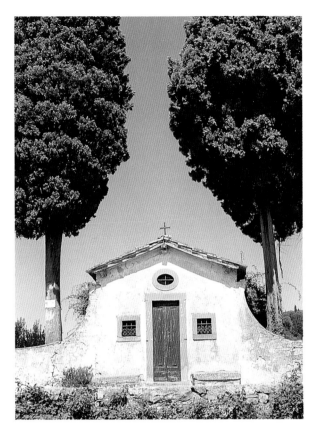

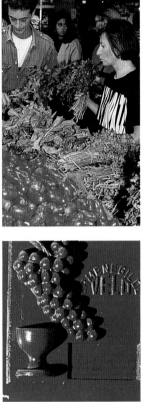

A research project called Chianti Classico 2000 has done much to help producers choose suitable clones, rootstocks and planting densities for each site as vineyards become due for replanting. The next challenge is quantifying and describing the variations in style from the area's different communes: San Casciano, Greve and its sub-zone Panzano, Barberino Val d'Elsa, Castellina, Radda, Gaiole and Castelnuovo Berardenga – variations of which the locals have long been aware.

A *consorzio* is a voluntary generic body set up to protect its members' interests. In the Classico zone there are two. The Consorzio del Chianti Classico is the legal watchdog, checking by tasting, analyses and vineyard and cellar visits that wines are in line with regulations, then issuing the pinky-purple DOCG neck labels that adorn all satisfactory wines. Anyone producing Chianti Classico needs to belong. The second is the Conorzio del Marchio Storico-Chianti Classico, the promotions and marketing body. The black cockerel (*gallo nero*) is its well-known symbol. Membership is voluntary and most producers belong, although several, some notably influential, prefer to remain outside. The Consorzio has set up a comprehensive web site, www.chianticlassico.com which has a wealth of detail on its members' estates. It also provides e-mail links to each.

Above left A tiny roadside chapel near Badia a Passignano in Chianti Classico.
Top Fresh tomatoes form the basis of much Tuscan cuisine.
Above Concrete vats have now been replaced on many estates by the more efficient stainless steel.

Small estate, concentrating on well-styled Chianti Classico. Vineyards adjacent. Modern art centre and open air museum. Book with estate.
Antinori
(See also Cantinetta Antinori in Florence.) *Tel: 055 23595*
Over 600 years old, in family hands and Italy's best-known and reputed company. Numerous estates in Tuscany (and adjacent Umbria). Carefully crafted wines of great appeal. Many produced including Chianti Classico, Badia a Passignano, Peppoli, Santa Cristina, plus famed super-Tuscans Tignanello (Sangiovese/Cabernet) and Solaia (mainly Cabernet).
Castello di Gabbiano
Tel 055 821053; fax: 055 8218082; E

Antica Fattoria Machiavelli
Large range: Annia (Sangiovese), R&R
(Cabernet blend), Ariella (Chardonnay),
Cabernet Sauvignon, Merlot,
Sangiovese; Chianti Classico Titolato:
normale, Riserva and Riserva Oro.
Book rooms 2-3 months prior.

Agricola Le Corti
Tel 055 820123;fax 055 8290089; E,F
Wines in transformation from rustic to
refined as year-on-year improvements
come to fruition. Chianti Classico only,
three versions. Superb old farm
buildings. Pay for tastings. Book rooms 6
months prior, via agency.

Fattoria Corzano e Paterno
Tel 055 8248179
Individual, love them or loathe them
wines. Chianti Classico normale and
Terre di Corzano Riserva, Il Corzano
(Sangiovese/Cabernet Sauvignon),
Aglaia (Chardonnay), Vin Santo.

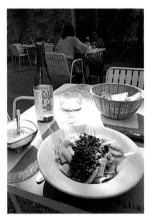

La Sala
Tel 055 828111
Rising star making juicy but persistent
Chianti Classico and Sangiovese/
Cabernet blend Campo all'Albero.

Fattoria Poggiopiano
Tel 055 8229629
Small, friendly estate; lively, characterful
Chianti Classico and Rosso di Sera
(Sangiovese).

HOTEL

Antica Posta (see opposite).

RESTAURANTS

San Casciano has plenty of good
places to eat. It is so close to Florence
that Florentines often drive out rather
than struggle through the city. Other
restaurants listed follow the wine route.

Antica Posta
Tel: 055 820116
Non-traditional but delightful. Light,

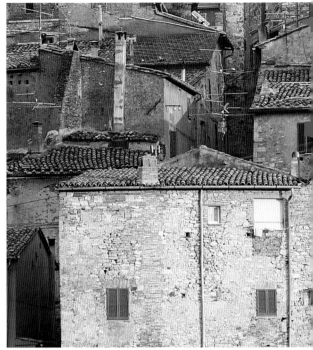

San Casciano

From the Firenze Certosa junction of the Firenze-Siena
superstrada just south of Florence, within five minutes you
can be rising into the first hills of Chianti Classico, at
Sant'Andrea in Percussina. This marks not only the earliest
glimpses of vines but, symbolically, the offices of the Chianti
Classico Consorzio. It may be worth a short stop to pick up
their detailed map, which is as useful for general touring as
it is for finding the locations of Consorzio members.

The offices are on the site of the old house of Machiavelli.
The Machiavelli museum is opposite. However – this is Italy
remember – the museum is run by the owners of the adjacent restaurant (see right), so, to visit it you need to turn up
around lunch or dinner time, otherwise it is closed. The
Machiavelli and Conti Serristori estates are just next door.

San Casciano, a couple of minutes' further along the road,
is a pleasant enough small town. There are a few estates to
the northwest along the road to Cerbaia, but the more
important ones are in the opposite direction. Generally,
though, the commune, with its white and yellow limestone
soils, is more important for olive oil production than for
wine, and olive trees dominate the scenery. If you look carefully, many will appear to have somewhat slim branches
sprouting from aged, thick trunks. These are the regrowths
from the dire frosts of 1985 (see p20).

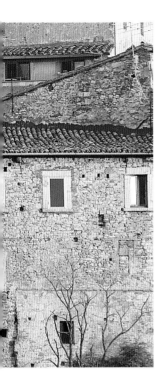

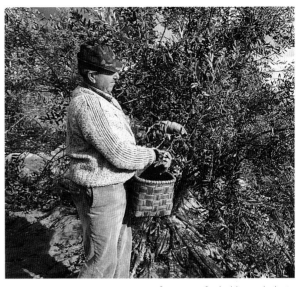

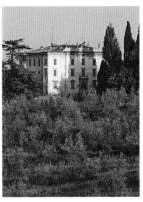

Above *San Casciano is a pleasant town and home to one of Italy's top restaurants, La Tenda Rosso.*
Left Pappardelle con ragu, *a pasta dish in* trattorie.
Top right and right *Olive groves around San Casciano. The area is the most important in Classico for olive oil.*

flavoursome food relying on the best local ingredients. Well chosen wines. Also a hotel. Closed Mondays.

La Tenda Rossa
(loc. Cerbaia; Piazza del Monumento, 9) Tel: 055 826132
One of Italy's top restaurants. A great experience for which you'll pay highly but not excessively. Finest ingredients combined into the most wonderful dishes. Superb wine list. Go, just go. Closed Monday lunch, Tuesday.

L'Albergaccio
Tel: 055 828471
Sant'Andrea in Percussina
Simple *trattoria*-style food. Also houses the Machiavelli museum. Cl Mondays.

Nello
(loc. San Casciano, Via IV Novembre, 64) Tel: 055 820163
Local, popular, family-run trattoria. Good Tuscan staples plus daily specials. Wines to match. Good value. Closed Wednesday pm and Thursdays.

Matteuzzi
(loc. Ponte Rotto, Via Certaldese, 8) Tel 055 828090
Family-run trattoria. Comforting food, good use of vegetables. Seats outside. Great value. Lunch only, except Fri, Sat, Sun. Closed Tue.

FOOD SHOPPING

Cooperativa La Ginestra
(loc Barsino, via Pergolato 3)
Full range of local produce (honey, oil, pasta, etc.), all organic.

For an idea of the life of the Tuscan nobility in the past, take a look at the Fattoria delle Corti Corsini, just on the right, a kilometre along the road to Mercatale. The solid, imposing-looking building has both cellars and an important *frantoio* (oil mill). A few minutes' further on, it is worth taking a short detour right to Montefiridolfi. There, swing right to see Fattoria La Loggia, an estate with over five centuries of history, or left for a glimpse of where Antinori's much-admired wine Santa Cristina is made. Back in Mercatale, go through the small town and shortly afterwards there is a crossroads. You could turn left (signposted Greve) for Castello di Gabbiano and the Castelgreve cooperative winery, but the road is unmade and not much fun if it's raining. It is better to go right (towards Panzano) on a road leading upwards through woodland, vines and olive groves. San Pietro a Sillano off to the left is a tranquil, pretty, privately owned church. But from here onwards you are in the commune of Greve.

Greve and Panzano

RECOMMENDED PRODUCERS

Villa Calcinaia
Tel: 055 854008 ; E, F
Owned by the Capponi family since the 16th century. Well styled, clean wines, especially Chianti Classico Riserva and Casarsa(Merlot). Pay for tastings. Book rooms with estate two months prior.

Castello di Verrazzano
Tel: 055 854243
Originally an Etruscan settlement. Bought by Verrazzano family in 7th century. Wine production documented in 1100s. Set high with great views. Rich, rounded wines: Chianti Classico Riserva, Sassello (Sangiovese), Bottiglia Particolare (Sangiovese/ Cabernet). Restaurant.

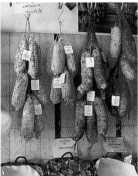

Castello Vicchiomaggio
Tel: 055 854079; fax: 055 853911; E, F, G
Impressive renaissance castle. Estate run with aplomb by John Matta. Well-knit, stylish wines led by Chianti Classico Riserva Petri, La Prima. Restaurant. *Agriturismo*: Book rooms with estate, 7 days minimum stay in summer only, preference given to wine-lovers. Banqueting rooms. Tastings at cost.

Riseccoli
Tel: 055 853598; E, F, G.
Firm, traditional Chianti Classico, ripe Saeculum (Sangiovese/Cabernet/ Merlot). Vin Santo. Business hours only. Direct sales. Olive oil. *Agriturismo.*

Castello di Querceto
Tel: 055 85291; E, G.
Set high, strategic site, great views. Owned for over 100 years by François family. Vineyards surround. Large range of wines led by Chianti Classico Il Picchio and La Corte (Sangiovese). Book rooms with estate two months prior, no minimum stay. *Agriturismo.*

O f all Chianti Classico's centres, Greve is the liveliest. The hub is the central piazza, and the highlight the *macelleria* (butchers) Falorni, which specializes in everything made from *cinghiale* (wild boar): from sausages to salami. To emphasize the point a (stuffed) wild boar stands guard outside. Just along from here is a small crafts shop selling, among other things, wine bottle stoppers adorned with Chianti's famed black cockerel. There are also a couple of wine shop *enoteche*.

Practically all Greve's estates are within 15 minutes' drive of the town; most are closer. Arriving from San Casciano, the first signed junction to the left after the church of San Pietro di Sillano leads in via Montefioralle. This is a superb medieval but Etruscan-looking village perched on a hill-top. Before taking that left turn, however, you might hop forwards to see the smallish but highly esteemed estate of Vecchie Terre di Montefili just half a kilometre ahead.

Leaving Greve northward is the Chiantigiana, the main road that winds right through Chianti Classico from south of Florence to Siena. Within five minutes you pass the estates Villa Calcinaia, Castello di Verrazzano and Castello Vicchiomaggio, on the left, all on classic *alberese* limestone soil.

Eastward from Greve the road is slower. The soil here has more sandstone and estates are less cheek-by-jowl, but follow the road towards Figline Valdarno and you will see

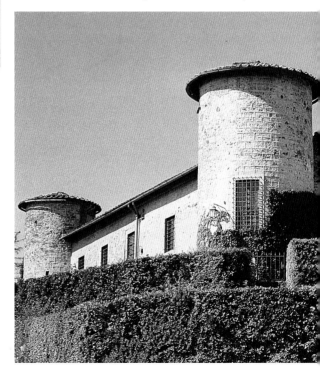

Riseccoli, Castello di Querceto and Carpineto. Heading south from Greve brings you onto a cool, wooded stretch of the Chiantigiana. Either follow it to Panzano, or fork left beyond Greve and turn immediately right onto a circular estate-hopping route which takes you past Savignola Paolina, owned by the Fabbri family for 200 years, Vignamaggio and 16th-century Castellinuzza. La Doccia, family-owned since the 16th century, follows, then Filetta and the 15th-century castle of Lamole (officially Lamole di Lamole, to distinguish it from the eponymous village), one of Greve's major fortresses.

Turning right shortly after passing Lamole (the estate) brings you into Panzano territory.

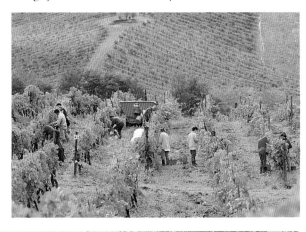

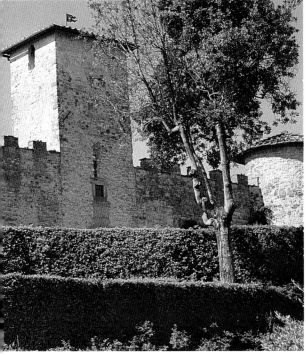

Carpineto
Tel: 055 8549062.
Comparatively new estate with a wide range of carefully made, well balanced reliable wines from other grapes and areas of Tuscany as well as the mainstay, Chianti Classico.

Agricola Querciabella
Tel: 055 853834
Full, rich, stylish wines of class and personality. Chianti Classico Riserva and normale, Camartina (Sangiovese/Cabernet Sauvignon), Batàr (Chardonnay) all good. Book.

Villa Vignamaggio
Tel: 055 853559
Carefully restored 15th-century villa with beautiful Italian garden. Winemaking records go back to 1400. Mona Lisa was born here. Three high ranking Chianti Classicos: normale, Riserva, Mona Lisa. Riserva rich, balanced and complex. Dry Vin Santo Olive oil. *Agriturismo.* Book rooms with estate 12 months prior, 2 nights minimum stay.

Lamole
Tel: 055 9501005
22ha of well sited vines.

Castel Ruggero
Tel 055 6819237
Small estate; text-book Chianti Classico.

La Madonnina - Triacca
Tel 055 858003
Up and coming estate. Chianti Classico normale, Riserva, **cru** La Palaia; Il Mandorlo (Cabernet), all well-structured and well fruited.

Podere Poggio Scalette
Tel 055 8546108; E, F
Owned by Vittorio Fiore, one of Tuscany's leading roving winemakers – so booking is essential. One wine, Il Carbonaione (Sangiovese), high quality, deep and concentrated.

Savignola Paolina
Tel 055 853139; E, F
Small, family run estate. Vineyards below house. Elegant and finely styled Chianti Classico plus Il Granaio (Sangiovese/Merlot). Visits business hours only. May pay for tastings.

Viticcio
Tel 055 854210
Concentrated, intense, powerful wines: Chianti Classico Riserva, Prunaio (Sangiovese), Monile (mainly Cabernet).

Far left *Falorni, the Greve butcher, specialising in boar.*
Main picture *On the way to Greve from San Casciano is the fortress of Castello di Gabbiano, overlooking the Greve valley.*
Top *A harvest scene in Chianti. Today openwork boxes are more commonly used to carry the grapes.*

Right Panzano, where a moderate climate and favorable soil result in some of the most refined Chianti Riserva.

PANZANO

RECOMMENDED PRODUCERS

Cennatoio
Tel: 055 852134
Hospitable 8 hectare estate. Reliably Good wines. Large range: Chianti Classico (3 levels); Etrusco (Sangiovese); Rosso Fiorentino (Cabernet); Mammolo-Merlot; red and white Vin Santo.

Castello dei Rampolla
Tel: 055 852001
Mid-sized estate with high-altitude vineyard famed for its use of Cabernet, firstly with Sammarco, now also with La Vigna di Alceo. Chianti Classico also good.

La Massa
Tel: 055 852701
Chianti Classico (normale, Girogio Primo) only, but both of great personality; particularly good in poor years.

Vignole
Tel: 055 592025
Welcoming; elegant Chianti Classico.

Le Masse di San Leolino
Tel: 055 852144
Owned by an Englishman, Norman Bain. Produces little but very good wine: elegant and firm.

Fontodi
Tel: 055 852006; fax: 055 852537; E, F
Fabulous estate; superb wines esp Chianti Classico Riserva Vigna del Sorbo and Flaccianello delle Pieve (Sangiovese). Book rooms with estate as early as possible.

Il Poggiolino
Sambuca Val di Pesa
Tel: 055 8071635
Well worth a detour to visit this friendliest of estates (Sambuca is signed right just after entering Greve commune). Open, rounded Chianti Classico.

Vecchie Terre di Montefili
Tel 055 853739; E
Smallish estate; acclaimed wines esp Chianti Classico, Anfiteatro (Sangiovese), Vigna Regis (Chardonnay/Sauvignon/ Traminer). Pay for tastings. Book.

Fattoria Casaloste
Tel 055 852725
Small, newish estate. Well-sited vineyards, especially cru Don Vicenzo. Completely organic. Only well-defined, stylish Chianti Classico. Must book.

Podere Le Cinciole
Tel: 055 852636
Bought in 1991 and now making attractive, fresh Chianti Classico normale and cru Valle del Pozzo Riserva. Vineyards in various sites.

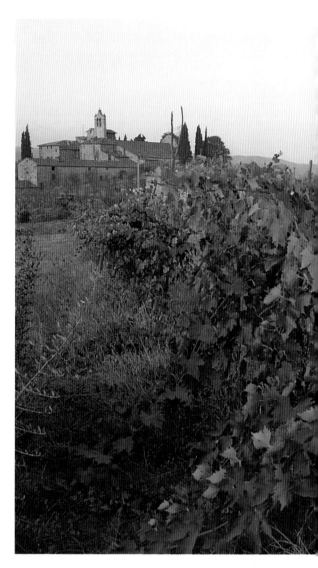

PANZANO

Panzano is officially a sub-commune of Greve but it is usually treated as if it were a commune in its own right. It is much calmer and quieter than Greve, having comparatively few people pounding its steep, narrow streets and it is one of Chianti's prettiest villages.

At the top of the hill is a well cared for church with a warden who just loves to get his face into photographs. The real draw to the village, however, is the *macelleria* Cecchini, a butcher's shop just down from the church, better known as Dario's. He draws customers from as far afield as Florence who come not just for the quality of the meat (Dario rears his own sheep) but also for the ready-prepared cuts, which can cater for smart dinners, large parties or even picnics. There is even clas-

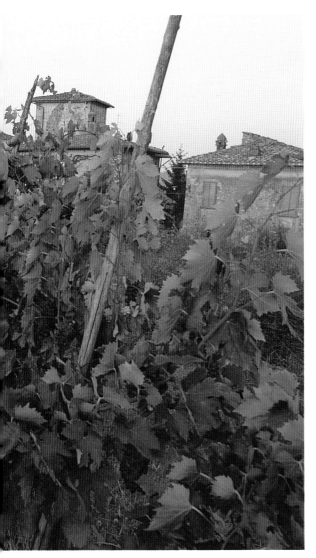

Le Fonti
Tel 055 852194
Tiny, boutique estate, high-sited.
Complex wines produced with
abundant tlc. Chianti Classico,
Fontissimo (Sangiovese/Cabernet).

HOTELS

Il Verrazzano
Greve, Piazza Matteotti, 28.
Tel: 055 853189
Simple, small, characterful, friendly
hotel. Also traditional trattoria.
Villa Sangiovese
Panzano, Piazza Bucciarelli, 5
Tel: 055 852461; fax: 852463
Attractive and comfortable. Pretty
rooms, some with good views. Pool.
Parking. Closed in winter.
Villa Le Barone
Panzano, Via S. Leolino, 19
Tel 055 852621; fax: 852277
16th century villa. Well furnished
rooms. Garden. Pool. Parking.

RESTAURANTS

Il Vescovino
Panzano, Via Ciampolo, 9/11
Tel: 055 852464
Interesting dishes competently
prepared. Well selected wines. Seats
outside; good views. Not expensive.
Trattoria del Montagliari
Panzano
Tel: 055 852184
On the estate premises: popular with
locals and Florentines. Hearty, meat-
based food, full of flavour. Not
expensive. Closed Mondays.
Giovanni da Verrazzano
Greve, Piaza G. Matteotti, 28
Tel 055 853189
Long-standing trattoria. Rigorously
Tuscan. Good choice of local wines.
Seats outside. Closed Sun pm, Mon.
Da Padellina
Strada in Chianti, Corso del Popolo, 54
Tel 055 858388
Long standing trattoria. Simple Tuscan
food, abundant portions. Excellent
meat. Large range of local wines.
Seats outside. Very good value.
Oltre Il Giardino
Panzano, Piazza G. Bucciarelli, 42
Tel 055 852828
Tuscan-based food. High-level wine
list. Seats outside, great views. Not
expensive. Closed Wed lunch, Tue.

ENOTECHE

La Cantinetta Greve
Bottega del Chianti Classico
Greve
Enoteca del Chianti Classico
Panzano
Enoteca Baldi Panzano.

sical music drifting across the counter. Panzano also boasts craft leather workers and a hand-made shoe craftsman.

Coming into Panzano from the Chiantigiana you pass Montagliari; coming in from Lamole you see Cennatoio. Once through the village, take a brief jaunt onwards, forking left onto an unmade road. A lane to the left brings you to Castello di Rampolla; an equally uncomfortable track takes you to La Massa and Vignole. Turn back to Panzano, go through the village once more and head southwest (towards Castellina). After a couple of minutes Le Masse di San Leolino appears on the left followed by the magnificent Fontodi, the last of the Panzano estates.

Looking back, you can see the village perched up to the right behind you.

Barberino

RECOMMENDED PRODUCERS

Isole e Olena
Tel: 055 8072763; E, F, G, Sp
Paolo de Marchi's painstaking dedication to his vineyards is unparalleled. He produces beautiful, intensely fruity wines of great character: some of

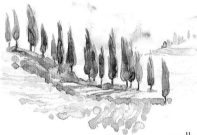

Tuscany's best. Cepparello (Sangiovese) is amazing, vibrant Chianti Classico brilliant, Vin Santo wonderful. Cabernet Sauvignon, Syrah, Chardonnay in same league. Cellar visits only. Must book.

Le Filigare
Tel: 0335 5752617; fax: 055 755766; It only
Small estate with finely structured Chianti Classico, Podere Le Rocce (Sangiovese/Cabernet) and others. Book with estate.

Casa Sola
Tel: 055 8075028; fax: 055 8059194; E, F, Sp
Mid-sized. Well made wines. Pay for tastings. Visits 10-12am, 4-6pm. Must book for vineyard visits. Book with estate 4-6 months prior.

Casa Emma
Tel: 055 8072859; E
Smallish estate. Rounded, well-fruited, intriguingly complex wines. Chianti Classico, Soloio (Merlot). Large groups must book.

Castello di Monsanto
Tel: 055 8059000; fax: 055 8059049; E
Wines stored in long, underground cavern. High quality, densely structured wines of long aging potential. Emphasis on Chianti Classico, especially Il Poggio Riserva. Also Nemo (mainly Cabernet), Fabrizio Bianchi (Chardonnay). Book.

Right *The characteristic charm of rural Tuscany.*
Far right *A flower-bedecked stairway leads to a village house in the commune of Barberino.*

The village of Barberino, officially Barberino Val d'Elsa, lies outside Chianti Classico but its commune stretches well inside and includes several major estates. It is easily reached from Panzano or Castellina and is a short distance from the San Donato exit of the Florence–Siena *superstrada*.

Arriving from Panzano turn right (or from Castellina, left) at the junction for San Donato. You pass through La Piazza, so tiny it has little to offer beyond an espresso. A couple of kilometres further on is Le Filigare, off to the left, the first Barberino estate. At the next junction take the left fork (signposted Castellina) for Barberino's heartland. The right fork leads into San Donato in Poggio, a sub-commune of Barberino, with an impressive 11th-century church. The hills are fairly steep and the territory mixed: vines, plenty of olive grove, pine forest. Many vineyards have excellent *galestro* soil.

The first track to the right leads to Villa Francesca; the second, to Casa Sola, lying about three kilometres further down. After these junctions you pass Casa Emma and Fattoria La Ripa. Then turn right towards Olena. From there continue straight along the narrow unmade road to Isole e Olena, Castello della Paneretta and Fattoria Monsanto respectively. These last two are castles in the true sense of the word: four-square, solid-built, strongly defensive structures. The rivalry between Florence and Siena today amounts to little more than a niggle or a light joke. In centuries past it led to years of serious warfare, and fortified castles were a necessary protection against invasion.

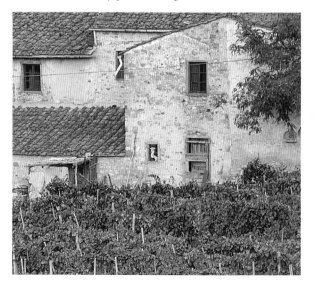

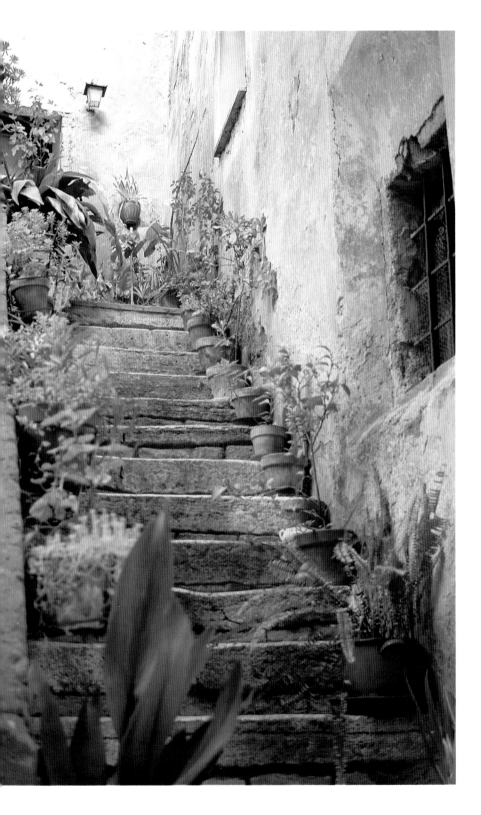

with estate 2 months prior.

Castello della Paneretta
Tel: 055 8059050; fax: 055 8059024;
E, F, G
15th century castle, restored in 17th.
Firm but elegant wines. Chianti
Classico normale, Riserva, Torre a
Destra Riserva. Quattrocentenario
(Sangiovese) released to commemo-
rate the castle's 400th anniversary. Le
Terrine (Sangiovese/Cabernet). Pay for
tastings. Must book. Book with estate.

CASTELLINA

RECOMMENDED PRODUCERS

Ruffino, Santedame
Tel: 055 83605
Enormous company based at
Pontassieve (Chianti Rufina) producing
large quantities of generic Chianti and
base Chianti Classico. Also has several
properties in Chianti Classico with high-
er, and increasing quality output. The
Santedame estate is notable for
Romitorio di Santedame (Prugnolo/
Colorino): deep, dark, punchy, powerful.
**Casavecchia alla Piatta di
Buondonno**
Tel & fax: 0577 749754; E
Small, family run estate. Chianti
Classico, Syrah. Large groups pay for
tastings. Must book 4-5 months prior,
min stay 3 nights.
Fattoria Nittardi
Tel & Fax: 0577 740269; E, F, G
Once on the Florence-Siena battlefront,
this was originally a massive fortress
called Nectar Dei. Run at one stage by
Michelangelo's nephew. Set in extensive
woodlands but just 11ha of vineyard.
Refined, classically styled Chianti
Classico Riserva and softer normale.
Book with estate or through agency.
Rocca di Cispiano
Tel: 0577 740961
High sited with superb views. Rich
ripe Chianti Classico and Rocca di
Cispiano (Sangiovese)
Castello di Fonterutoli
Tel: 0577 740476; fax: 0577 741070;
E, F, G
In a small, perfectly preserved
medieval hamlet. Run by the Mazzei
family since 1435. Finely textured,
complex, concentrated wies of
immense class. The starry Castello di
Fonterutoli, Chianti Classico Riserva
leads range. Also Fonterutoli Chianti
Classico, Siepi (Sangiovese/Merlot),
Badiola (Sangiovese). Pay for tastings.
Must book. On-site trattoria. Book
through agency 6 months prior.
Castello di Lilliano
Tel: 0577 743070
Large estate, medieval layout, owned

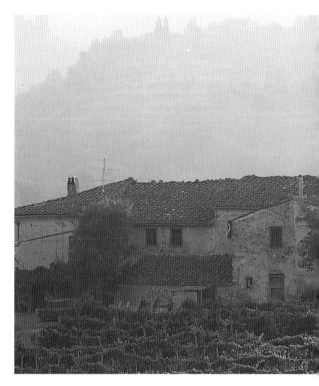

Castellina

If Chianti Classico is the heart of Chianti then Castellina,
luxuriating in the full title Castellina in Chianti, is the
heart of the heart. The commune has more open countryside than Greve or Barberino with even the odd grassy field;
the scenery is softer, and the vine-covered hills come in
beautiful flowing sweeps giving gasp-worthy views. Vines
grow mainly on *alberese* or sandstone but there are outcrops
of clay, quite heavy in parts. There are also some magnificent rows of cypress trees lined up like tin soldiers. The
cypress trees usually appear in pairs, either an array of them
lining the driveway to an important property, or as a single
pair: the traditional way to mark land ownership boundaries.

Castellina is a 15–20 minute drive along the Chiantigiana
from Panzano; it takes a similar time from the San Donato
exit of the Florence–Siena *superstrada*. It is also reasonably
close to Poggibonsi and San Gimignano (see p74), to Radda
(see p58) and not far from Siena. You can eat well there,
drink well and find plenty of pleasant places to stay
overnight: in short, the perfect centre.

The town has a quiet, confident air, busy without bustle.
The central piazza is tiny, but the streets running off it mix
shops, businesses and houses with calm ease. Behind the
main street is the long covered corridor of Via delle Volte.

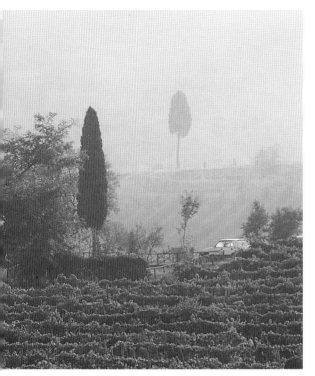

Main picture *Dawn mist envelopes a Chianti farmhouse and vineyard.* Below *Fresh ravioli, made with a variety of stuffings.*

by Principi Ruspoli. Good, traditional firm wines. Several levels of Chianti Classico plus Vigna Catena (Merlot).

Rodano
Tel: 0577 743107
Mid-sized, family run estate. Elegant, well-fruited Chianti Classico, normale and Viacosta Riserva. Also Monna Claudia (Sangiovese/Cabernet).

Tenuta di Bibbiano
Tel: 0577 743065; fax: 0577 743202; E, F, G, Sp
Mid-sized estate on an old Etruscan site. Vines grown in 11th century. Big, powerful, concentrated, characterful wines: Chianti Classico Montornello and Riserva Vigna del Capannino. Visits business hours only. Book with estate 6-8 months prior.

San Fabiano Calcinaia
Tel: 0577 979232
On an old medieval site of which

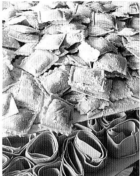

traces remain. Vineyards on two sites: San Fabiano, Cellole. Finely tuned, stylish, full, well balanced, long lived wines of class. Chianti Classico normale and Cellole Riserva; Cerviolo Rosso (Sangiovese/Cabernet).

Rocca delle Macie
Tel: 0577 7321; fax: 0577 743150; E, F, G
Large complex in a tiny 14th-century hamlet. 250ha of vine with additional grapes bought in. Large quantities of good value, everyday Chianti Classico and other staples plus far smarter Chianti Classico Riserva Fizzano, Ser Gioveto (Sangiovese), Roccato (Sangiovese/Cabernet). Large groups pay for tastings. Book with estate, 2-day min stay in winter.

Castellare di Castellina
Tel: 0577 742903; fax: 0577 742814; E, F

On one side are the backs of buildings, the other side looks over Chianti. Castellina is built on a ridge 550 metres high, and the view is breathtaking.

It is worth tracing two routes from the town: Castellina north, and Castellina south and southwest (this latter known as Castellina Scalo). If you have followed the Panzano and Barberino routes and arrived from San Donato/Barberino you will have covered some of Castellina north already. Nevertheless retracing the route in the other direction gives the countryside a completely different look.

The north route leads out of Castellina on the Chiantigiana past Casanova di Pietrafitta on the left, then Il Faggeto and Quercetorta (both left) and Pietrafitta on the right. A forested, vine-free stretch leads to the San Donato junction. Take this left fork and after La Piazza you can take either the 'main route' or the 'short cut'. The former takes you past Poggio al Sorbo and slices through part of Barberino. Follow signs to Castellina to emerge back in Castellina at a turn-off to Ruffino's Santedame estate and a minute later, a lay-by (right). The 'short-cut' is only half the distance but takes one of Chianti's famous 'white roads' (unmade, narrow, and bumpy) so it will take twice as long and could be twice as much fun. After La Piazza turn left (towards Nittardi). You pass Buondonno and shortly after, a side road to Nittardi, then you meander through the countryside until you emerge at the same lay-by as on the 'main

Mid-sized estate. Reliably good, refined, 'quiet' wines. Wide range. Chianti Classico normale, Riserva, Riserva II Poggiale; I Sodi di San Niccolò (Sangiovese/Malvasia Nera), Coniale (Cabernet), Canonico (Chardonnay), Spartito (Sauvignon), Vin Santo.

Podere La Brancaia
Tel: 0577 743084
Fine, complex, slow-developing wines well-reflecting vintage and origin. Chianti Classico, Brancaia (Sangiovese/Merlot).

Tramonti
Tel: 0577 741205
Small, new, American-owned. Just Chianti Classico (so far), fussed over like a new baby.

EATING OUT

Albergaccio di Castellina
Loc. Albergaccio, Via Fiorentina, 35
Tel: 0577 741042; eves only Tue-Thu, cl. Sun
Well known and reputed rustic restaurant. Traditional food, notably main dishes, starters with individual touches. Good cheeses. Broad ranging, wine list well put together. Seats outside. Cash only. Not cheap but good value.

Antica Trattoria La Torre
Piazza del Comune, 15
Tel: 0577 740236; cl. Fri

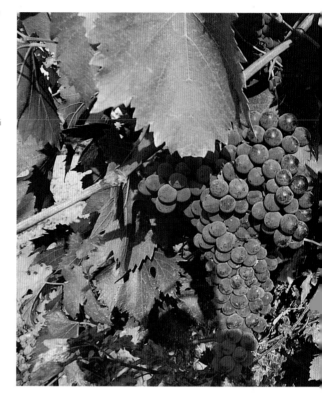

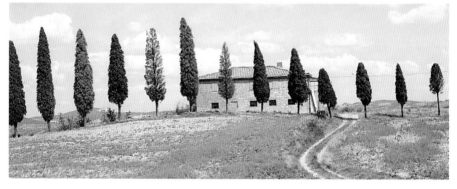

Main picture (top) *Canaiolo is an official constituent of the Chianti blend, but is being used progressively less as, according to current thinking, the more Sangiovese in the blend, the finer the wine.*
Above *Cypress trees form a dramatic boundary across the top of a Tuscan hill.*

route'. The view over western Chianti here is magnificent with San Gimignano distinctly visible in clear weather. Head back into Castellina over the Macia Morta, a 600-metre-high ridge.

For the southern route, leave Castellina on the Chiantigiana towards Siena. Passing Il Villino and Tregole to the left, five minutes more brings you to the peaceful hamlet of Fonterutoli, much of it connected with winemaking for the Castello di Fonterutoli estate and most of it owned by the estate's noble Mazzei family. The road then skims the corner of the commune of Castelnuovo Berardenga (see p66). Take a sharp right at the next junction onto an

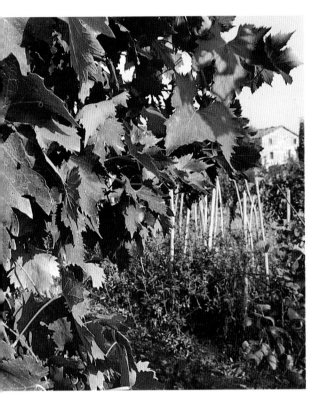

Long-standing, family-run trattoria, always busy. Ample portions of simple, local fare, well cooked and flavoursome. Fair range of local wines. Seats outside. Inexpensive.

Osteria di Fonterutoli
Loc. Fonterutoli
Tel: 0577 740476
On eponymous wine estate. Local dishes handled with a light touch, cooked to mouth-watering perfection. Drink estate's wines.

HOTELS

Salivolpi
Via Fiorentina, 89
Tel: 0577 740484; fax: 0577 740998
Designed as traditional Tuscan country house. Well appointed rooms. Gardens. Pool. Parking. Good value 3*

Villa Casalecchi
Loc. Casalecchi, 18
Tel: 0577 740240; fax: 0577 741111
Converted 19th century villa. Richly furnished rooms, all different. Good bathrooms. Extensive gardens. Swimming pool. Parking. 4*

Tenuta di Ricavo
Loc. Ricavo, 4
Tel: 0577 740221; fax: 0577 741014
Tranquil, comfortable rooms in renovated medieval farmhouses. Good bathrooms. Good restaurant. Extensive gardens. Pool. Parking. Good level 4*.

ENOTECHE

Enoteca il Cantuccio
Enoteca Orlandi
Enoteca Le Volte
Bottega del Chianti Classico

unmade road, past Le Galozzole (with sales point) to San Leonino. The castle visible on the left as you approach is Fortezza di Tuopina. This is a particularly pretty part of the commune: open, soft and with panoramic views, including one of Tuscany's most majestic rows of cypress trees which you will see shortly. A little further on the impressive Lilliano site practically blocks the road. Scoot round behind it and head west (towards Poggibonsi), another section with wonderful views. You pass the castle of Bibbiano on the left then rise rapidly to Rodano and descend to San Fabiano Calcinaia. The estate buildings are situated just outside the Chianti Classico border, so turn back and at Lilliano head left over a narrow rutted road towards Rocca delle Macìe, one of Chianti's largest estates. From there you can amble back to Castellina at your leisure.

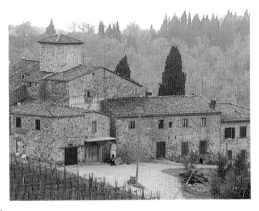

For another fix of the countryside, you could make a third trip. Turn sharp left just through Castellina, passing Cellole to see respectively Castellare, Rufone, Brancaia, Villa Rosa, Picini and Gretole. From there you could continue to Poggibonsi and San Gimignano – or turn back.

Above A farmhouse near Castellina in Chianti. Vines in this part of Chianti grow on alberese or sandstone but there are outcrops of clay in parts.

Radda

RADDA

RECOMMENDED PRODUCERS

Fattoria dell'Aiola
*Tel: 0577 322615; fax: 0577 322509;
E, F, G*
Originally 13th-century fortified castle.
Destroyed on Siena front line in 16th,
rebuilt as pretty villa. Welcoming mid-
sized estate. Full, warm, well-fruited
wines. Large range. Must book for
vineyard visits.

Fattoria Terrabianca
Tel: 0577 738544; E, G
Swiss-owned 17th century
farmhouse, completely modernised.
Chunky wines. Shop with oils,
conserves etc as well as wines.

Podere Terreno
Tel: 0577 738312; fax: 0577 738400
15th century farmhouse. Friendly and
welcoming estate. Soft, all too
drinkable wines: Chianti Classico,
normale and Riserva; Pierfrancesco

Below *Vagliagli is small, tranquil
and very pretty, an ideal spot for a
gentle stroll.*

The commune of Radda in eastern Chianti is one of Chianti Classico's highest, with some estates at an altitude of over 600 metres. There are some pretty steep slopes and roads often follow hill ridges. There is also plentiful woodland with more deciduous trees than further west, and there are even a few areas of scrub. The soil is darker, red-tinged in parts, although *alberese* dominates south of the town with sandstone in the higher areas to the north.

Radda town is a disappointment. It is marred by an unsightly brick depot at its southern end and, although its centre is quite pretty, it lacks the personality of Castellina or Panzano. It is, though, where the Consorzio Chianti Classico (see p45) was founded in 1924: the spot where their offices were sited (by the Relais Vignale) is marked by a plaque.

Radda is best reached from Castellina. There is a fairly direct route (10–15 minutes) eastward, but it has no particular wine interest. The longer route, a glorious twisting and heavily wooded road, is a much better choice. Head out southward from Castellina on the Chiantigiana and branch left after five minutes onto an unmade road signposted Vagliagli. A few old granite wheels, once used for crushing olives, lie along the roadside and all is overlooked by the hamlet of Fonterutoli up to the right. There are 'necropoli

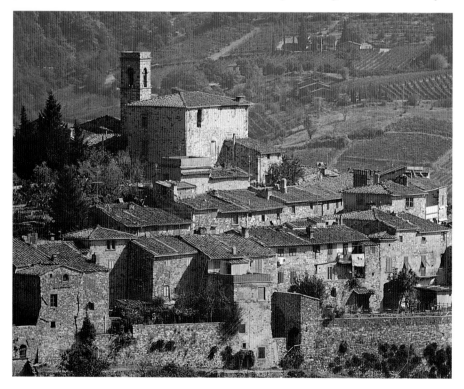

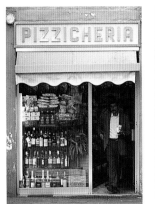
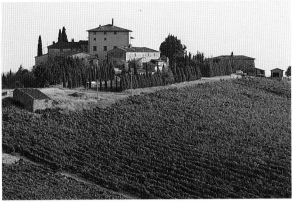

etrusca' signposted (right) but unless you have a four-wheel drive it is better to reach this small Etruscan burial ground on foot. The next estate up on the left is Tregole. The road snakes up and down, then onto a ridge with better views, including Quercegrossa down in the valley to the right.

At the entrance to Vagliagli, before turning left to go through the village, take a detour down the slope and right, then left after about 100 metres. This leads to a wonderfully peaceful, forested lane, a 'protection oasis' (protected from hunting) and eventually to Dievole, a large, modernistic wine estate. Vagliagli itself is a small, pretty hill-top village despite the horrors of trying to pronounce its name, and is well worth visiting if only for a leg stretch.

Head back north towards Radda, first passing Aiola then Terrabianca before an estate-free saunter into the town. From Radda there are a few out-and-back routes possible, all easily completed in half a day. The route not to be missed, though, is a round trip. At the first crossroads through the town turn left, then right a couple of kilometres further along. The next fork is the beginning (and end) of your circle. Fork right and you rise through the typical Chianti combination of vineyard, olive grove and wood to Podere Terreno (right) and Pruneto (along a lane to the left) then, a few minutes later, Volpaia. The church on the left is Santa Maria Novella; you will pass it on your return.

The cluster of buildings that makes up Castello di Volpaia is almost a village in its own right. Apart from cellars, wine-making areas and a *frantoio,* there are workmen's houses, a church, even a small general store and bar – with excellent coffee. (Watch where you park if you stop here as there are often consignments of wine being moved about.) Continuing upwards, after a couple of large leftwards bends, turn left at the T-junction and head back down, passing Castelvecchi and the Santa Maria Novella church, an area of outstanding natural beauty and with the beautifully preserved, serene Volpaia in full view across the valley.

Once back down at the T-junction, turn left towards

Above left The name Pizzicheria *is special to Florence and its environs but most small towns have at least one shop selling cheeses and salumi with other foodstuffs.*
Above Radda's vineyards tend to be on steep slopes. Buildings are on hill tops - a legacy of its war-torn past.

(Sangiovese/Cabernet) Business hours only. Pay for tastings if not buying. Book rooms with estate 3 months prior, min. stay 2 nights, half board.

Podere Pruneto
Tel & fax: 0577 738013; E, F
Tiny estate, family-run, welcoming (despite the guard dog). Just Chianti Classico of high level. Can visit without booking. Book rooms with estate, 1-4 months prior, min. stay 3 nights.

Castello di Volpaia
Tel: 0577 738066; fax: 0577 738619; E, F
One of Chianti's most highly sited and most highly regarded estates. Powerful, assertive, rich, long-lived wines. Chianti Classico, normale and Riserva; Coltassala (Sangiovese/ Mammolo); Balifico (Sangiovese/ Cabernet); Vin Santo; Torniello (Sauvignon/Semillon); Bianco Val d'Arbia. Pay for tastings. Must book. Cookery courses. Book rooms with estate 1 month prior; min stay 2 nights in winter.

Fattoria di Montevertine
Tel: 0577 738009; fax: 0577 738265; E, G
Owned by the jovial Sergio Manetti. Run by son-in-law Klaus Remitz. Eschews Chianti Classico; eschews 'foreign' varieties. Who cares? The wines are terrific: Montevertine Riserva, Il Sodaccio, Pian del Ciampolo (all Sangiovese/Canaiolo), Le

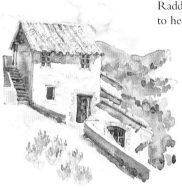

Radda but at the next junction go left again (instead of right to head into town). On this road there is no shortage of vines or estates. Huge swaths of vineyard on your left accompany your descent. A couple of minutes further along a lane on the left leads up steeply to Monte Vertine, an estate situated high on a ridge, with the most glorious of views over the Chianti hills. Just past the Monte Vertine cut-off is Poggerino (right).

The next track to the left leads up to the hill-top Podere Capaccia, just across the valley from Volpaia, with views as good as those from Monte Vertine. The property centres on a remarkably well preserved medieval hamlet, but beware, the road up is poor and steep, and may be hard work for a small car and very much so if the road is wet. Forking off the track is Crognole.

The next estate, after another few minutes, is Castello d'Albola, with its two fat towers emerging powerfully from the centre of a mass of *poderi* (small farms or plots), each with its own small farmhouse. This was the pattern of most estates during the *mezzadria* (see p9) but now each *podere* and accompanying house are owned outright. Albola itself, once out of sight of those daunting towers, is a glorious, quiet little place with harmoniously restored estate buildings. It is also Radda's northernmost estate, so it is time to turn back.

Pergole Torte (Sangiovese). Excellent whites too: Bianco di Montevertine, M (both Trebbiano/ Malvasia). Pay for tastings. Visits pm only. Book rooms with estate at least 2 months prior.

Poggerino
Tel: 0577 738232
Gem of an estate, small and friendly. 13th century origins. Wines, just from Sangiovese, made with great care, complex, well-fruited. Chianti Classico normale, Riserva, Bugialla Riserva.

Podere Capaccia
Tel: 0577 738385, book on 0574 582426; E, F, G (but weekends and August only!)
Very small estate; high quality, intense wines: Chianti Classico, Querciagrande (Sangiovese), Spera di Sola (Malvasia/ Trebbiano). Pay for tastings.

Castello d'Albola
Tel: 0577 738019; E
Great views: site used by BBC for filming. Ancient cellars. Owned by the huge Zonin group and large (150ha) but concentrated, refined wines made with great care: Chianti Classico Riserva, Acciaiolo (Cabernet/ Sangiovese), Le Marangole (Pinot Nero), Le Fagge (Chardonnay), Vin Santo.

Livernano
Tel: 0577 738353
New estate with fixed ideas. No Chianti. Instead Puro Sangue (Sangiovese), Nardina (Cabernet/ Merlot), Livernano (Sangiovese/ Cabernet/Merlot), Anima (Chardonnay/Sauvignon/Traminer).

Agricola Monterinaldi
Tel: 0577 733533; E, G
Quite large with well-sited vineyards. Finely structured wines. Chianti Classico, normale and Riserva; Pesanella (Cabernet/ Sangiovese); Gotizio (Sangiovese/ Canaiolo); Vin Santo; Monterinaldi Bianco (Chardonnay/ Trebbiano). Business hours only. Large groups pay for tastings.

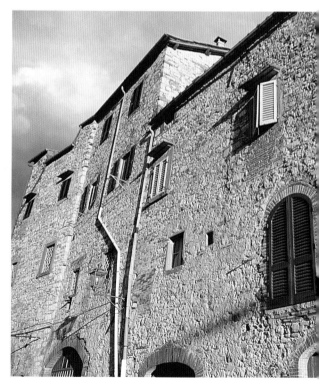

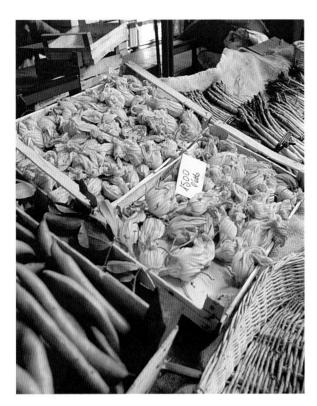

HOTELS

La Locanda
Loc. Montanino
Tel & fax: 0577 738833
Tiny, but idyllic. Restored farmhouse.
Welcoming; comfortable rooms. Great
views, shady terrace, gardens, pool.

Relais Fattoria Vignale
Radda, Via XX Settembre
Tel: 0577 738300; fax: 0577 738592
For effortless self-indulgence. Calm
rooms, traditionally furnished but with
all mod. cons. Gardens, pool. Vignale
restaurant adjacent.

Vescine Il Relais del Chianti
Loc. Vescine
Tel: 0577 741144; fax: 0577 740263
Converted medieval hamlet.
Traditionally styled and furnished.
Comfortable rooms. Good
bathrooms. Pool. On-site restaurant.

RESTAURANTS

Vignale
Via XX Settembre, 23
Tel: 0577 738094; cl. Thu
Good quality ingredients. Home
made pasta, bread. Well flavoured,
well balanced dishes. Large, mainly
Tuscan wine list. Well respected.
Good service. Expensive.

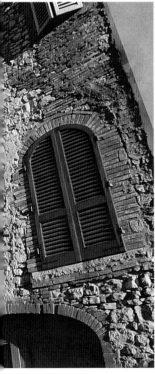

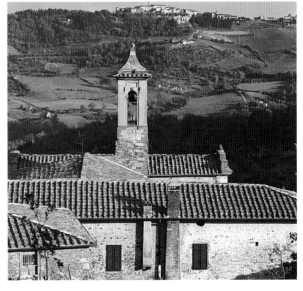

Left *The stone façades of buildings
in Radda have a soft, warm glow.*
Top *Spring is the season of delicate
zucchini (courgette) flowers, broad
beans, sometimes eaten raw in
salads, and asparagus.*

Above *The hill top town of Radda
can be seen in the background,
overlooking the convent of Santa
Maria. Radda has some beautifully
preserved old buildings which include
several wine estates.*

Le Vigne
Tel: 0577 738640
For the sheer pleasure of dining right in the middle of a vineyard.

ENOTECHE

Enoteca Castello di Vagliagli
L'Arte del Vino
Dante

FOOD SHOPPING

Enoteca/Paninoteca
Combined wine and bread shop – inspired thinking
Gastronomia/Enoteca Porciatti
Wide range of salumi, other high quality foodstuffs, delicatessen, ready-to-eat dishes. Locally renowned.
Pasticceria Sampoli & Lapis
'Caffè Sandy'

PLACES OF INTEREST

Ceramics from:
Le Ceramiche di San Bernardo
Vagliagli, Via Chiantigiana
Angela Piamgiam
La Malpensa, Radda
Ceramiche Rampini
Radda-Gaiole road

GAIOLE

WINE PRODUCERS

Castello di San Polo in Rosso
Tel: 0577 746045; fax: 0577 746153; E, G
Beautiful castle, completely renovated. Small church with many frescoes. Underground cellars. Firm, refined wines of staying power. Chianti Classico, normale and Riserva; Cetinaia (Sangiovese) and others. Pay for tasting. Must book. Book rooms with estate.
Castello di Ama
Tel: 0577 746031
Large estate. High quality, stylish, individualistic wines; much admired. Three Chianti Classico crus plus normale. Also series of varietals, Merlot, Pinot Nero, Sauvignon etc.
Agricoltori del Chianti Geografico
Tel: 0577 749489; E, F
An exemplary cooperative winery is like. Wines made from 450ha of members' vineyards. Four levels of Chianti Classico, all well made, all good value. Pay for tastings. Must book.
Barone Ricasoli
Tel: 0577 7301; E, F
Situated in Brolio, Gaiole's most magnificent castle. Large. After some ups and downs in recent years now back on course. Powerful, concentrated yet softly fruited wines. Chianti Classico

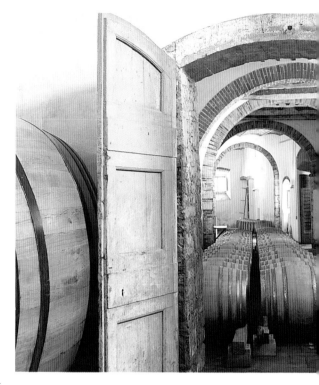

Gaiole

Gaiole village is small, little more than a single street, and rather uninspiring although it does boast an *enoteca* and a couple of places to eat. It is only five kilometres southeast of Radda, but even the most direct road is two to three times as long. Additionally, some of its estates are as close to Radda as to Gaiole, so the best starting point for any Gaiole tour is Radda. The area can be seen comfortably in half a day.

Leave Radda the way you first arrived, but at the junction for Vagliagli and Lecchi, turn towards Lecchi. Almost immediately fork right up to a pretty, tranquil church, San Giusto in Salcio. You get good views of Radda from its spacious terrace, which is ideal for a quick sandwich.

Moving south into Gaiole territory the terrain becomes quite mixed. The soil is practically all *alberese* in this western part (there's sandstone in the east) and vineyards abound. There is also a gradual increase in olive cultivation. A long track on the right leads to the impressive San Polo in Rosso and another, almost immediately after, rises along a curved ridge to Castello di Ama. (Follow the signs for 'Fattoria di Ama', not just 'Ama' or 'Casanuova di Ama', which is a separate estate.) Castello di Ama is large and functional yet blends well into the countryside. Even if you do not plan to stop, it is worth driving right round the complex for the 360-degree views of the countryside.

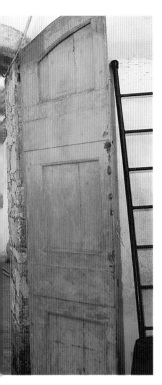

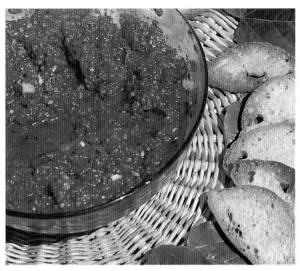

Above Bruschetta al pomodoro, *a local speciality – bread topped with a tomato sauce.*

Two views of the large estate Rocca di Castagnoli: the cellars (left) *and* (below) *the* rocca *(fortress) itself.*

Just before Lecchi, an ideal Tuscan town in miniature, there is an almost perfectly conical hill to the left, with the village of Monteluco nestling within it. Past Lecchi towards San Sano, it gets flatter and wilder and Mediterranean pines start to appear. A few minutes past San Sano, another pretty, well-served village, the road curves left dramatically, then stops abruptly at a T-junction. To go straight into Gaiole, go left, but the tour continues to the right, into increasingly wild terrain. Turn left to Monti at the next set of signposts and you join the Strada dei Castelli del Chianti. This part of the commune was on the front line in the Florence – Siena

Brolio and Riserva Rocca Guicciarda; Casalferro, Formulae (both Sangiovese); Torricella (Chardonnay); Vin Santo. May pay for tastings. Must book (unless tasting only required). Book with agency.

Rocca di Castagnoli
Tel: 0577 731004
Large property, well rated. Wide range.

Rietine
Tel: 0577 731110; fax: 0577 738482; E, F, G
Smallish with well-made, mid-weight wines. Chianti Classico normale and Riserva, Tiziano (Merlot), Bianco (Malvasia/Trebbiano). Also grappas. Can visit any day of week. Book rooms with estate 3 months prior.

Fattoria Valtellina
Tel: 0577 731110
Full, concentrated, powerful wines. Chianti Classico, normale and Riserva; Convivio (Sangiovese/Cabernet).

Badia a Coltibuono
Tel: 0577 749498; E, F.
A monastery for over 700 years, now owned by the Stucchi Prinetti family. Wines from mature vines, complex and long lived, and among the area's most renowned. Chianti Classico normale and Riserva, Sangioveto (Sangiovese) and others. Shop. Restaurant. Cookery school.

Riecine
Tel: 0577 749098; E
Small estate. Fine yet austere, rich and intense yet elegant wines. Excellent Chianti Classico normale and Riserva. Also La Gioia (Sangiovese).

S M Lamole e Villa Vistarenni
Tel: 0577 738186; E, F, G
Two merged estates, Lamole with classic styled wines and Villa Vistarenni, where cellars are housed,

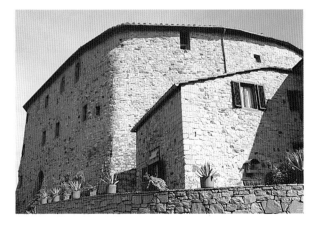

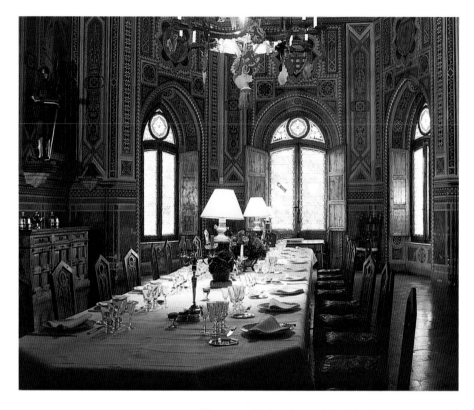

with softer, more forward wines. Four styles of Chianti Classico plus Codirosso (Sangiovese), Vin Santo, Bianco Val d'Arbia. Business hours only. Pay for tastings. Accomodation run separately from estate.

Rocca di Montegrossi
Tel: 0577 747267; fax: 0577 747157; E, F
Of 8th century Lombard origin; strategic point in Florence-Siena wars. More recently part of Castello di Cacchiano but now independent. Fleshy, fruity wines with firm backbone. Chianti Classico normale and Riserva Vigneto San Marcellino, Geremia (Sangiovese), Vin Santo. Pay if tasting full range of wines. Arrange vineyard visit when booking. Book rooms with estate 3-5 months prior.

HOTELS

Residence San Sano
Fraz. Lecchi, Loc. San Sano
Tel: 0577 746130; fax: 0577 746156
Group of renovated *case coloniche*. Attractive, relaxing rooms. Restaurant for hotel guests only. Pool. Parking. 4*
L'Ultimo Mulino
Loc. La Ripresa di Vistarenni
Tel: 0577 738520; fax: 0577 738659

wars. The many high points, with wide views, were natural defences. Gaiole *castelli* are castles indeed and well fortified.

At the first T-junction past Monti turn right (left leads to Podere Il Palazzino). Almost immediately to the left is the lane to Castello di Cacchiano's cypress-lined driveway, steep, but with fantastic views from its daunting castle.

The imposing Castello di Brolio soon rears up ahead. The original Chianti 'recipe' was laid down here almost two centuries ago by the owner, Barone Bettino Ricasoli. The cellars and winemaking plant are easily visible from the road. Turn left at the next junction, then right at the next, branching off the Gaiole road onto a 'white road'. After a short while Rietine appears to the left and then the 11th-century Rocca di Castagnoli ahead. Take the next left and four estates follow in quick succession. First is Rocca di Castagnoli (right), then Rietine (left). The unusual village of Rietine is worth a look: it was planned as a series of rings centred on the church. Next is Giorgio Regni (left) and finally, atop a stately, cypress-lined driveway, the heavily set, fortressed Castello di Meleto. Follow the road down. The buildings you pass are Meleto's cellars. Turn right at the T-junction to reach, finally, Gaiole town.

There is another cluster of estates north of the town, high, on quite different terrain. If time is short, go straight through Gaiole (direction Montevarchi), heading for the first major

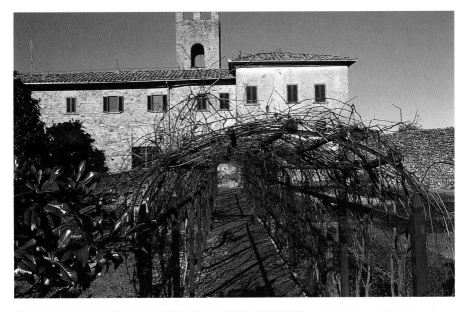

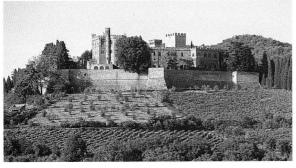

Far left *Some of Gaiole's castles are just as imposing inside as out. This is in Brolio.*
Above *The clear light of a crisp winter day highlights the outlines of the villa of Badia a Coltibuono.*
Left *Castello di Brolio – as classic a castle as any in Chianti.*
Below *Necks of Chianti Classico carry a DOCG approved sticker.*

Converted medieval mill. Gardens. Well-furnished, well appointed rooms. Good bathrooms. Pool. Parking. 4*.

EATING OUT

Osteria del Castello
Loc. Brolio
Tel: 0577 747194; cl. Thu
Pretty restaurant. Short menu based on fresh local produce. Shortish but

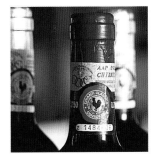

three-way junction (about five kilometres). Otherwise, leave Gaiole westward (left) part-way through the town on an unmade road towards Spaltenna. Shortly before the end of this twisting cut-through, with its extraordinary views of sandstone ridges, is Castello di San Donato in Perano.

Turn right at the end (towards Montevarchi), and climb to the three-way junction you could have reached directly from Gaiole. The left turn is to the leading estate of Badia a Coltibuono, 630-metres high and unmissable; the right turn (towards Gaiole) leads you to Tiorcia and Riecine. (For Riecine take the first lane to the left, then first right.)

This almost completes Gaiole, so go back along the ridge towards Radda. Eventually the view opens out and you come to a junction. You are practically back at Radda but, before heading right into town, turn left for Gaiole's (perhaps Chianti Classico's) most august view: the château (no other word quite describes it) of Vistarenni perched up in the hills at the end of a long, cypress-lined driveway leading from the road (it takes a good four minutes to drive along it). Majesty indeed.

Castelnuovo Berardenga

well chosen wine list. Seats outside.
Not expensive; very good value.
Il Carlino d'Oro
Loc. San Regolo, Via Brolio
Tel: 0577 747136; lunch only, cl. Mon
Long-standing, family-run. Short menu,
local dishes, home-cooked style. Good
choice of local wines. Cheap. Cash only.
**Panificio Pasticceria Gelateria
Bianchi Guido**
The complete self-indulgence kit:
bread, pastries and ice cream.

ENOTECA

Rinaldi Palmira, L Lecchi

FOOD SHOPPING

Paolo Ciolini, Lecchi
Wide range of foodstuffs and wines
Gastronomia Bianchi, Gaiole
Good delicatessen

**CASTELNUOVO
BERARDENGA**

WINE PRODUCERS

San Felice
*Tel: 0577 359087; fax: 0577 359223;
E, F, G*
Large estate, beautifully cared for.

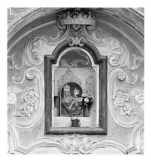

Largish range of wines, high and ever-
improving quality; concentrated,
rounded and well-balanced. Three
levels of Chianti Classico, led by Poggio
Rosso Riserva; Vigorello (Sangiovese/
Cabernet); two whites. Pay for tastings.
Must book. Book c/o Hotel (see pXX).
Villa Arceno
Tel: 0577 359346
Up and coming estate. Good Chianti
Classico, especially cru Vigna La Porta.
(See also under Hotels.)
Fattoria di Felsina
Tel: 0577 355117; E, F, G
Also known as Felsina Berardenga.
Guiseppe Mazzocolin, intelligent,
studious but with a delicious sense of

Castelnuovo Berardenga is Chianti Classico's southernmost commune. The countryside is not unlike southern Gaiole (which almost bisects it) with its open, sometimes wild, sometimes restful views, but there is a warmer feel to the surroundings and the olive is in greater evidence. Soils are quite mixed. The town itself is outside the Classico zone and has the comfortable feel of a quiet, local hub.

It is not difficult to reach from Gaiole, although it could take over half an hour, but for a tour of its estates it is best to start from Siena or Castellina. This route assumes Siena: if you are coming from Castellina you will need to read backwards. The roads are quite fast, so half a day is ample time to allow.

From Siena (or the Florence–Siena *superstrada:* Castelnuovo is about an hour from Florence) heading towards Arezzo, fork left at the Asciano turn-off, go through

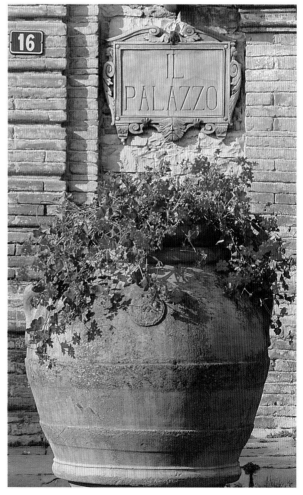

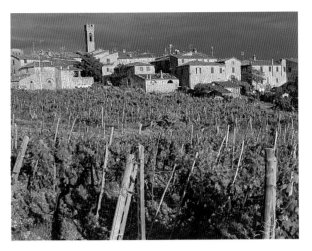

humour and his friend, consultant Franco Bernabei, are making wines to die for. Refined, powerful, complex and characterful, these are the pace-setters. Chianti Classico Riserva cru Rancia and Fontalloro (Sangiovese) lead the team but Maestro Raro (Cabernet), I Sistri (Chardonnay), even the normale Chianti Classico and the fresh white Pepestrino (Trebbiano, Chardonnay, Sauvignon) are all excellent. Top class oil too. Advise when booking to see vineyards. Tasting in estate's own enoteca.

Castello di Bossi
Tel: 0577 359330
Up and coming estate. Small range led by Chianti Classico Berardo Riserva.

Castell'in Villa
Tel: 0577 359074; fax: 0577 359222; E, F, G, Sp, Grk
Owned by Greek Princess Pignatelli della Leonessa, this largish estate makes individualistic but consistently good wines. Heavy concentration on Chianti Classico (three levels) but also Santacroce (Sangiovese/Cabernet), Vin Santo. Pay for tastings. Business hours only. Good restaurant in hamlet serving estate's wines (eves only, cl. Mon). Book rooms with estate; min stay 3 nights.

Allegretti
Tel & fax: 0577 355756; E, F
Small estate. Well-sited vineyards, organic cultivation. Produce Chianti Classico and cru Vigna del Capanno del Ramerino, Vin Santo, olive oil. Must book. Book with estate 2 months prior. Just one apartment in converted hay loft, comfortable, in traditional Tuscan style.

Castello di Selvole
Tel: 0577 322662
Vineyards stretch along a well-exposed ridge at 450m. Direct sales. Major enterprise with swimming pool, tennis and volley-ball courts, mountain bike hire.

Poggio dell'Oliviera
Tel: 0577 322652
Tiny estate but good wines.

Valiano
Tel: 0577 356850
Large, 225ha property, dotted with traces of Etruscan settlements. Extensive olive groves. Direct sales.

Le Trame
Tel: 0577 359116
Tiny estate, just Chianti Classico, produced with boundless love and care. Firmly structured, concentrated, well-balanced, good character.

Montaperti and into the vine-covered hills of Chianti Classico. Looking behind, you'll catch magical glimpses of the Siena towers. At the first major junction turn right towards San Felice and eastern Castelnuovo. Bossi appears on the right after a couple of minutes. Next is San Felice, which is a joy. Although dominated by the estate it is a perfectly cared-for *borgo* (hamlet) with its own piazza, church and *frantoio*. Turn right at the first junction past San Felice (if coming from Gaiole you join here) and proceed to Villa a Sesta, which is well worth exploring.

San Cosma lies just before the next junction, a hub for two short visits, San Cosma is on the right. Here, turn left to San Gusmé, then right to Villa Arceno. This is a huge, magnificent property, one of very few which was neither broken up, nor changed by the passing of the *mezzadria* (see p9) and gives a remarkable insight into the importance of such estates in the rural economy. Workers' houses are scattered widely around the august villa and its cellars, stables, granary, etc. The houses are now being converted to *agriturismo* apartments.

Back at the 'hub' junction take the road ahead, south towards Castelnuovo Berardenga town. A little over three kilometres down is Felsina, right on the Chianti Classico border but producing some of the zone's best wines.

At the 'hub' once more, take a sharp left (southwest). Just a few minutes brings you to a hefty gateway on the left with a long drive: the approach to Pagliarese, with Castell'in Villa next door. The comparative warmth of the area is revealed by its thriving umbrella pines.

Before long, you arrive back at the tour's starting-point, but carry on westward, to Pianella and the Arbia river, the bisection point of Castelnuovo. On maps the Arbia is prefixed 'T' for *torrente* rather than 'F' for *fiume* (river). It usually looks more like a dribble but, when in spate, can become a torrent indeed, as the smashed bridge over the Arbia frighteningly displays.

Fattoria di Petroio
Tel: 0577 328045; E
Small, family-run estate. Juicy, fruity, all
too drinkable Chianti Classico,
normale and Riserva.

HOTELS

Hotel Villa Arceno
Loc. San Gusmè
Tel: 0577 359292; fax: 0577 359276
Restaurant eves only, open 7 days.
17th century country lodge. Well
appointed, relaxing rooms, traditionally
furnished, with views. Very good
bathrooms. Gardens. Pool. Garage. 4*.
On-site restaurant has elegant but
relaxed atmosphere. Choose between
local and non-Tuscan dishes, both from
fine ingredients and prepared with skill.
Wines to match High quality but costly.

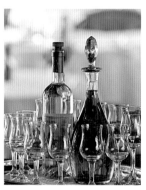

Relais Borgo San Felice
Loc. San Felice
Tel: 0577 359260; fax: 0577 359089
Wonderful tranquil atmosphere, in
restored medieval hamlet. Tastefully
furnished rooms. Excellent bathrooms.
Sheer luxury. Pool. Garage. Top level
4*. Restaurant, Poggio Rosso, always
open. High quality, refined dishes. Large
wine list. Seats outside. Seriously costly.

EATING OUT

Enoteca Bengodi
Via della Società Operaia, 11
Tel: 0577 355116; cl. Mon
Huge wine list, mainly Tuscan.
Seasonally changing menu. Local dish-
es, good use of vegetables. Choice of
olive oils. Inexpensive, good value.

Above *Only a few wine producers
in Tuscany make grappa; Vin Santo
is the traditional post-prandial
drink.*
Above right *Vines in Castelnuovo
Berardenga, Chianti Classico's
southernmost commune, benefit from
the comparative warmth of the area.*

Fine estates are less concentrated in western Castelnuovo
but the scenery is possibly even better. Almost immediately
on the left is a cypress-lined driveway to Vitignano and,
butting out into the road, Macia. After climbing for a further few minutes there is a sign to the *ruderi* (ruins) of the
Castello di Ceretto although little now remains. Neither are
they easy to find.

The next estate on the right is Monteropoli. Continue
past the small church of Asciata then, as the road bends left,

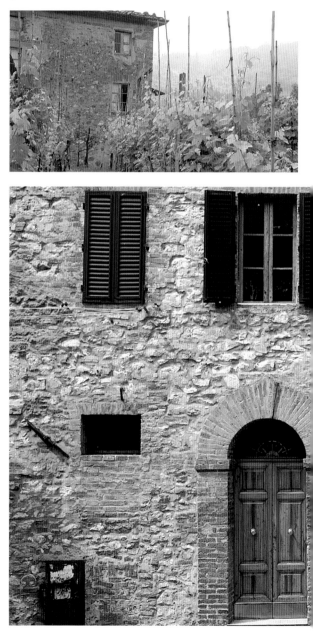

up to the right is Castello di Selvole, another big complex centred on a beautiful villa with splendid views. Unusually its approach is attractively lined by olive trees instead of cypresses.

At the next cluster of road signs you could take a quick detour left to see Borgo Scopeto, although the entrance may be closed, revealing nothing more than a glimpse of villa behind a mass of olives. Otherwise head onward before taking a sharp V-shaped turn down to the left. Immediately on your right is Poggio dell'Oliviera. In the next few minutes you pass near Vigna a Sole, Fattoria Corsignano and then Valiano, another major property, and catch sight of the Certosa di Pontignano across to the left. Towards Valiano, a seemingly aimless avenue of cypress trees appears. It's only looking back that their path becomes clear. Fattoria Il Castagno appears a minute later on the left, and after a further minute you meet the Siena–Castellina road.

Turn right. You soon pass Podere Olmo and within the batting of an eye the last curves of Castelnuovo Berardenga are behind you. You are now at Quercegrossa (in the Castellina tour).

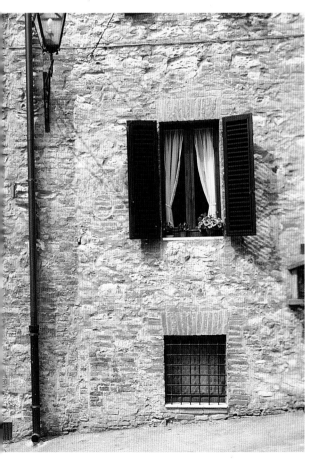

Da Antonio
Via Fiorita, 38
Tel: 0577 355321; eves only, cl. Mon
A real and welcome change, a fish restaurant – good too. Fish very fresh, choice of simple or more complicated dishes. Tasting menu. Large, wide ranging wine list. Service a bit wobbly. Seats outside. Very popular. Fairly priced.
La Bottega del Trenta
Loc. Villa a Sesta
Tel: 0577 359226; eves only, cl. Tue, Wed
Unusual. In old house with old furnishings, few tables. Eccentric owner, otherwise friendly service. Innovative dishes, with light touch, from local ingredients. Well selected wines mainly local. Fairly priced. Cash only.
Vecchia Osteria
Loc. Ponte a Bozzone, Via della Certosa, 15

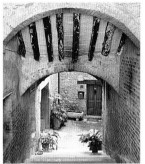

Tel: 0577 356809; cl. Sun
Small elegant restaurant. Seats outside. Local ingredients, dishes based in tradition but with inventive touches. Good wines. Fair value.
Villa Arceno
See under Hotel Villa Arceno.
San Felice,
Poggio Rosso
See under Relais Borgo San Felice.

FOOD SHOPPING

Macelleria Pini, Minucci
Castelnuovo Berardenga
Two good butchers.
Pasticceria Lodi e Pasini
Castelnuovo Berbardenga
Mouth-watering pastries.
Caseificio La Fonte di Torre a Castello
Excellent local cheeses.

Castelnuovo Berardenga (left and above) *lies just outside the Chianti Classico zone but is bigger than other similar commune centres and has an unassuming and friendly atmosphere.*

Siena

Below The Campo, lying just outside the original city walls, is where carriages and carts were unloaded and their wares taken to market.

Siena is a significant staging post on any wine tour of Tuscany not just for its own delights but for its proximity to most of the major wine areas. Chianti Classico's more southern communes, San Gimignano, Montepulciano and Montalcino, can all be reached within an hour's drive and it is a good start-off point for many of the region's important non-wine towns and villages too.

The city is inextricably linked with the *Palio* (see p73), but also very proudly displays its foods, wines, culture and historical warrior prowess from its commanding hill-top position.

Arriving at Siena from any direction is a memorable experience as its famous twin towers hive into view, sometimes from a great distance, at other times, not until you are within a couple of minutes of the outskirts. Siena's roads weave back and forth in elegant but disorientating curves across the hills, both inside and outside its compact, traffic-free centre. It is, however, surrounded by plentiful car parks and there is a good bus system if you park further afield.

Inside, steps and slopes line the twisting cobbled streets. These are crowded during the *passeggiata* (evening stroll), but when dinner-time arrives they empty within minutes.

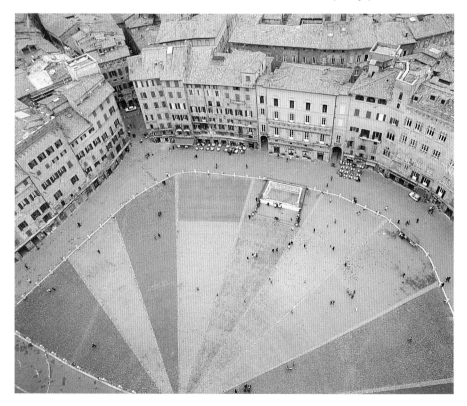

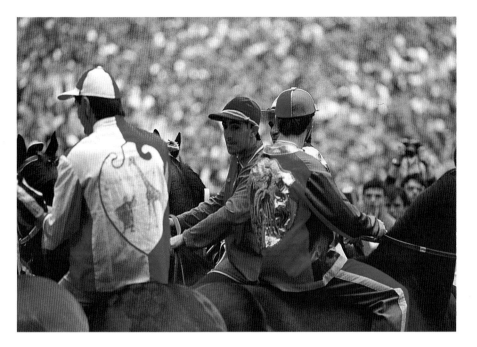

In winter the city can then take on the aspect of a ghost town, the narrow streets dark and shuttered – making arrival at the Campo or the Duomo eerily exciting. In summer there is much more life. Even so, it is quieter after dark than one would expect, with folk making merry in *trattorie* and restaurants rather than on the streets.

Siena is divided into 17 *contrade* (very roughly tiny boroughs), each of which has its own shield, colours and flag. Rivalry between the *contrade* is intense and reaches unbelievable levels during the *Palio*. A good selection of plates and plaques and so on, decorated with the colours of each *contrada*, are available to buy.

ENOTECA ITALIANA

Also known as the Enoteca Permanente, the Enoteca Nazionale, the Enoteca di Siena and La Fortezza, the Enoteca is a vast collection of hundreds of wines from all over Italy, beautifully presented in a vaulted cellar inside the old Medici fortress. It is not a complete collection, though. Producers choose whether to have their wines displayed, and pay an annual fee, as long as a tasting committee is satisfied. Naturally, the collection is strongest in Tuscan wines. Above the cellar is a spacious area for tasting and drinking with a non-smoking zone. There are tables outside in the summer, and sometimes a piano bar.

Every day a couple of wines are suggested for tasting but any wine on display is available by the glass. Cold snacks are on offer too. All wines can also be bought as off-sales. Opening hours are noon to 12.30 a.m.

Above *Rehearsal for the* Palio. *If lucky, you may see flag-tossing in the Campo. Even better, street dinners are held and visitors can buy tickets. Ask at the tourist office.*

Certosa di Maggiano 4*
Strada di Certosa, 82
Tel: 0577 288180; fax: 0577 288189
Park Hotel Siena 4*
Via Marciano, 18
Tel: 0577 44803; fax: 0577 49020
Villa Scacciapensieri 4*
Strada di Scacciapensieri, 10
Tel: 0577 41441; fax: 0577 270854

EATING OUT

Osteria Le Logge
Via del Porrione, 33
Tel: 0577 48013; cl. Mon lunch, Sun
Characterful restaurant popular with academics. Book-lined walls. Generous portions of 'personalised' Tuscan dishes with a light touch. Good, mainly Tuscan wine list. Try owner's own Montalcino.
Il Ghibellino
Via dei Pellegrini, 26
Tel: 0577 288079; cl. Mon
Popular. Simple food, well cooked, from good ingredients. Short menu, changing regularly. Shortish but well balanced wine list. Good house too. Good value.
Castelvecchio
Via Castelvecchio, 65
Tel: 0577 49586; cl. Tue

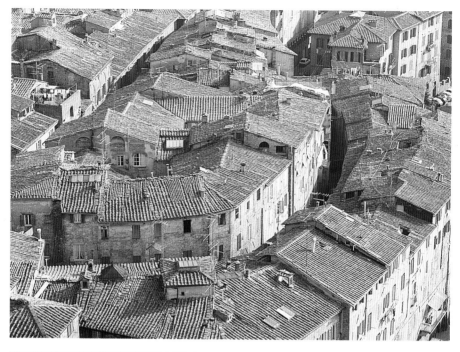

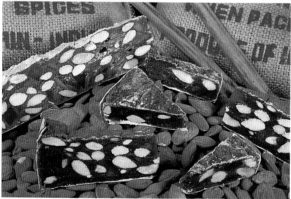

Above *Siena's elegantly curved streets are steeply sloping or stepped.*
Left *Siena's famous* panforte: *a spicy mix of candied fruit and nuts.*
Right *The Duomo dominates Siena's skyline.*
Far right *Siena is wonderful for shopping, notably for food and wine.*

(winter), 1.00 a.m. (summer). (Tel: 0577 288497.) The Fortezza is well signposted but street lighting sometimes fails. Take a torch.

FOOD SHOPPING

Siena has many speciality food shops, seemingly far too many for its size. Most Sienese, though, buy food at the daily market, behind the Campo in Piazza del Mercato. Siena is known for its sweetmeats, especially *ricciarelli*, rich almondy, marzipan biscuits; *panforte* ('strong bread' packed with almonds, dried fruit and spices, and totally indulgent); and *cantuccini*, crisp, almond-flavoured, almond-studded biscuits, ideal for dunking in Vin Santo.

PLACES OF INTEREST

The Campo

You can't not visit the Campo. The sloping, shell-shaped 'square' is lower than its approaches so your first view is practically panoramic and far better than any photo. Outside

Former stables. Great use of vegetables; totally vegetarian menus twice a week. Home made pasta. Great meat. Good wine list, knowledgeable staff. Value.
Da Enzo
Via Camollia, 49
Tel: 0577 281277; cl. Mon
Fish- or meat-based menu. Good, eclectic wine list. Fairly priced.
Mariotti da Mugolone
Via dei Pellegrini, 8
Tel: 0577 282235; cl. Thu
More traditional than this it is hard to find. Good choice of Tuscan wines. Fairly priced.
Taverna del Capitano
Via del Capitano, 8
Tel: 0577 288094; cl. Tue

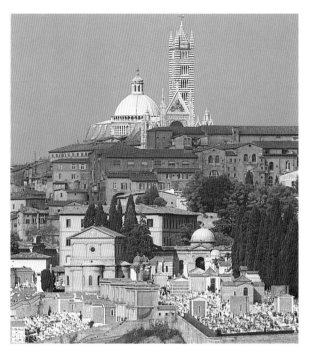

Attractive restaurant. Typical Sienese food, well flavoured, well cooked. Large, mainly Tuscan wine list. Value.
Hosteria il Carroccio
Via del Casato di Sotto, 32
Tel: 0577 41165; cl. Wed
Small, family-run trattoria. Weekly changing menu, based on local ingredients and dishes. Tasting menu (abundant). Shortish but well selected wine list. Very good value.
Osteria Le Chiacchiera
Costa di S. Antonio
Tel: 0577 280631; open 7 days

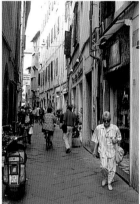

Tiny, pretty trattoria. Classic dishes, tasty and comforting. Small wine selection. Very popular. Great value.
Vinaio Trombicche
Via delle Terme, 66
Tel: 0577 288089
For good but inexpensive snacks in city centre (and for people watching).
Antica Trattoria Botteganova
Strada Chiantigiana 29
Tel: 0577 284230; cl. Mon
On the Siena-Gaiole road. Beautifully planned and executed dishes, light and flavoursome. Good service. Fine wine list to match. Not expensive.

FOOD SHOPPING

Drogheria Manganelli
Via di Città, 71/73
Extensive specialist grocery. Large selelction of local wines.
Gastronomia Morbidi
Via Banchi di Sopra, 75
Delicatessen famous for foods and dishes made on the premises.
La Nuova Pasticceria
Via Dupré, 37
The tops in Sienese sweetmeats.

the original city walls it was the medieval market day 'car park'. Now it is dominated by the 14th-century Palazzo Pubblico, topped by the Mangia tower. This symbolised the power of the laity over the church and was craftily built just higher than the cathedral's tower. Unless a meal with a view is essential, avoid eating in the Campo, as you will pay heavily for the experience.

The Duomo

This is just a minute or so from the Campo. Some people adore the 13th-century striped cathedral, others loathe it. Either way, its Piazza is hardly big enough to do it justice.

The *Palio*

It seems impossible that a horse race, run three times round the Campo and lasting just over a minute, can so dominate a city. Yet the Palio whips Siena into a frenzy, and tales of skulduggery abound. Ten of the 17 *contrade* compete: the seven excluded the previous year plus three chosen by lot. The race itself is terrifying. Not only are riders both suicidal and murderous in their intent to get round first (coming second is the greatest ignominy), but the diabolical San Martino corner regularly sees some off. Spectators are packed so tight it's scarcely safer for them; far better to watch it on television. Still, it is all accompanied by much feasting and the street dinners, before and after the event, are worth seeing if nothing else. The *Palio* is held twice a year, in early July and mid-August, with practice runs on the days before.

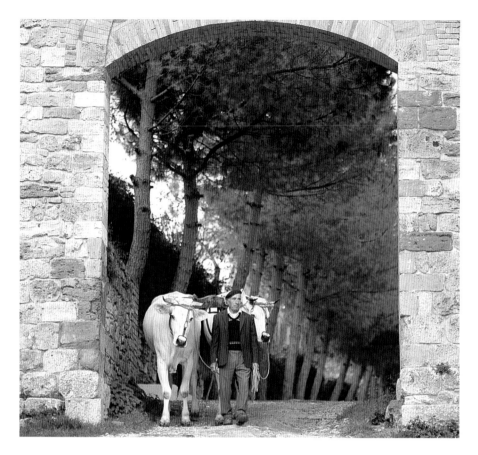

Above *A romantic view of rural life around San Gimignano – a man stands at the gates to the town with his cows.*

SAN GIMIGNANO

WINE PRODUCERS

Casale-Falchini
Tel: 0577 941305; E, F
Visits 9-11, 14-16 weekdays only.
Structured, well perfumed wines.
Vernaccia Vigna a Solatio and oaked
Riserva AB Vinea Doni, Chianti Colli
Senesi, Vin Santo, Falchini Brut
(sparkling) and others.

Teruzzi e Puthod
Tel: 0577 940143, E, F, G
Officially entitled Fattoria Ponte a
Rondolino. Run by Milanese Enrico
Teruzzi and his French wife, ex-
ballerina Carmen Puthod. Widely
acknowledged as the zone's best
estate. Rich, fruit-laden Vernaccias,
normale and Vigna Rondolino (with
10% Chardonnay); Terre di Tufi (80%
Vernaccia, oaked). Also Carmen

San Gimignano

San Gimignano is the one place that does not fit conveniently into a round tour of Tuscany. It is, though, still easily accessible. You could take a day out from Chianti Classico, or visit from Florence or Siena, or come from Volterra to the west. Whichever way, it can be reached in less than an hour and the 'city of towers' itself is so spectacular that it is tempting to see it sooner rather than later. In addition, although better known for its white wines, the San Gimignano area lies within the Chianti Colli Senesi zone, so it is probably best seen before exploring further south and west.

GETTING THERE

Unless you approach from Volterra you will need to get through Poggibonsi, an ugly, semi-industrial town with nothing notable except frequent traffic jams. If coming up from Siena, take the old Via Cassia, the second state road created by Mussolini, from Rome to Florence. It is slower than the *superstrada* but much prettier and gives great sights of the ancient castle of Monteriggioni. Once past

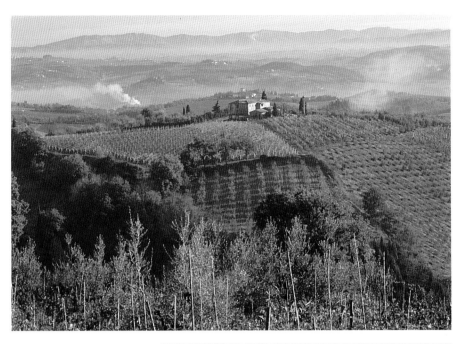

Poggibonsi the road starts to rise from the Elsa valley, giving the first glimpses of San Gimignano.

There are now has just 13 towers in the town of San Gimignano although there were once more than 70. It seems that in the middle ages, the higher your tower, the greater your prestige, so each family tried to outdo its neighbours, building ever higher (with the inevitable occasional col-

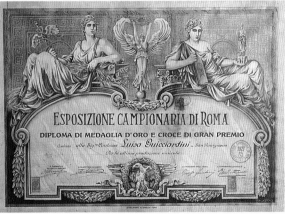

lapse). The towers also provided the means of spying on neighbours and came in handy for launching missiles in the all too common event of a feud.

Top *On clear days distant mountains can be seen from San Gimignano.*
Above *A plaque adorning a cellar.*

THE WINES

Vernaccia is a white grape variety whose name can be roughly translated as 'belonging here' so it is not surprising that records show it growing in the area around San Gimignano from the 13th century. Depending on how it is handled the wine can be deeply coloured, broad, rich and flat; or almost colourless, fresh, clean but rather neutral in flavour. The skill is in finding the balance between the two. Producers' ideas on the balance point vary and there are notable differences in the wines' styles. Things have now

(Sauvignon), Peperino (Sangiovese). Pay for tastings. Must book.
Montenidoli
Tel: 0577 941565; E, F
Friendly estate. Highly individualistic, elegant wines. Three Vernaccias, Fiore, Tradizionale, Carato (oaked). Unusual rosato (Canaiolo). Sono Montenidoli (mainly Sangiovese).
Panizzi
Tel: 0577 941576; E, F
San Gimignano's new star. Mid-sized, emphasis firmly on vineyard

75

techniques. Tight, slow-developing Vernaccia; normale and oaked Riserva. Also Chianti Colli Senesi and others. Visits business hours only. Must book.

Pietrafitta
Tel: 0577 943200
Firm, slow-developing, characterful wines.

Pietraserena
Tel: 0577 940083
Elegant Vernaccia normale and cru Vigna del Sole. Also good Chianti Colli Senesi Poggio al Vento and others.

Fattoria Cusona - Guicciardini Strozzi
Tel: 0577 950028; E, F
Mid-sized, centuries old estate. Four Vernaccias: normale, cru San Biagio, Perlato (with Chardonnay), Riserva (oaked). Red Millenni (mainly Sangiovese) produced to celebrate estate's 1000th anniversary. Visits weekdays only. Must book.

Casa alle Vacche
Tel: 0577 955103
Finely tuned wines. Three Vernaccias: normale, I Macchioni, Crocus (oaked). Good, ripe Chianti Colli Senesi.

Baroncini
Tel: 0577 940600
Large company, with quality leaping upwards. Several styles of Vernaccia. Intriguing La Faina (Trebbiano Toscano). Promising sparkling wine.

Mormoraia
Tel: 0577 940096
Converted convent with picture-book views. Distinctive wines, all oaked: Vernaccia, Ostrea (Vernaccia/ Chardonnay), Neitea.

Il Palagio
Tel: 0577 953004; E (slight)
Large estate, in imposing castle, recently acquired by large company Zonin. Well made, well fruited Vernaccia, Chianti Colli Senesi and Sauvignon. Office hours.

Above right San Gimignano takes on a gentle, welcoming aspect in the rich light of early evening.
Below Flowers are plentiful in the charming town centre.

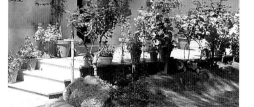

been complicated further by many producers opting to have three different styles: a 'pure' Vernaccia, one with a proportion of Chardonnay (sanctified by the DOCG regulation), and an oaked version. Many producers make red wine too; San Gimignano lies within the Chianti Colli Senesi zone, although not all opt to make use of this denomination.

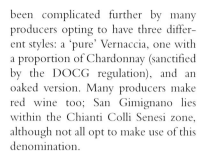
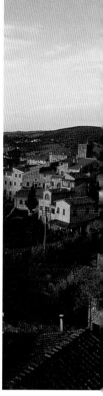

THE VINEYARDS

Soon after spotting San Gimignano, you get glimpses of its first vineyards.

The estate Pietrafitta is the first you will pass, well signposted, although the cellars are off a small side-road to the right. Others quickly follow as you head up to the hill-top town. The area around Pietrafitta and those closest to the town should, in theory, produce the best wine but with the Vernaccia grape the hand of the winemaker often has a greater effect than small zonal fluctuations.

As the climb continues, the plots of vineyard become more dense and the city views more vivid. San Gimignano is, in fact, situated only a little over 300 metres high, but it seems much higher.

The enclosed centre is necessarily traffic-free, but there are several car parks as you approach. Or you can skirt the centre, keeping the city wall on your right, and just as you leave it behind there is a soft curve down with space to park on the verge. This is also the start-off point for a round tour of some of San Gimignano's idyllic, vine-immersed countryside.

Follow the road down in the direction of Certaldo to a Y-shaped junction where you fork left. Later the road sweeps round to the right in a large U-shape and leads towards Ulignano, passing the estates of Pietraserena (to the right), Casale-Falchini (left) and Teruzzi e Puthod's Ponte a Rondolino. At the next T-junction turn left (not to Ulignano) and continue on a winding descent to the following T-junction. There turn left again. This leads down to the northern extremity of the San Gimignano area by the Elsa valley, skirting Certaldo, where the difference between the pretty old town above and the mundane town

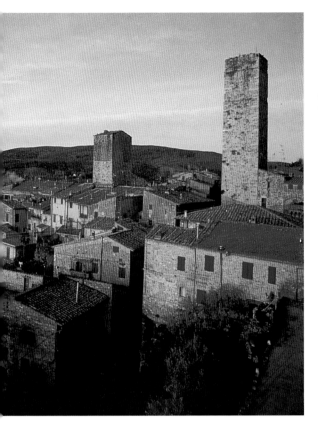

ENOTECHE

Fiaschetteria di Boboli
Becucci Gustavo
(or Bar Enoteca Chianti Classico). Great
range of wines. Hearty cheap snacks.
Il Castello
La Casa del Caffè
Wine and food.
Vecchi Sapori

HOTELS

La Cisterna
Piazza della Cisterna, 24
Tel: 0577 940328; fax: 0577 942080
Centrally located 14th century building
with good views. Comfortably furnished
rooms. Parking. Good value 3*.
La Collegiata
Loc. Strada, 27
Tel: 0577 943201; fax: 0577 940566
16th century building set in large
gardens. Fine rooms with period
furniture. Pool. Parking. Good level 4*
Villa San Paolo
Strada per Certaldo, km4
Tel: 0577 955100; fax: 0577 955113
In pretty, art nouveau villa set in large
gardens. Large, well-furnished rooms.
Pool. Parking. 4*
Bel Soggiorno
See under Eating Out below.

EATING OUT

Osteria del Carcere
Via del Castello, 13
Tel: 0577 941905; cl. Wed
Good spot for a glass and a snack at
any time, or full meals. Salumi and
meat supplied by the famed Dario of
Panzano but good vegetable options
too. Good range of wines by glass
and bottle. Good value. Cash only.
Bel Soggiorno
Via San Giovanni, 91
Tel: 0577 940375; fax: 943149; cl. Wed
Restful restaurant; great views. Locally
based dishes. Good wine list, not just
Tuscan. Fairly priced. Also attractive,
comfortable, good 3* hotel. Parking.

FOOD SHOPPING

Buca di Montaiuto,
Via San Giovanni, 16
Good salumi, especially from wild boar.
Casa del Caffè,
Via San Matteo
Wine and foodstuffs.

PLACES OF INTEREST

Pieve di Cellole
Glorious, small, simple medieval
church on Certaldo road with
cypress-lined approach.

below is a salutary lesson in town-planning. Then take a
sharp U-turn southward, back up towards the town, passing
Fattoria Il Paradiso, San Quirico (with the Pieve di Cellole
nearby) and Le Colonne further up on the higher slopes.
Half an hour should be enough time to complete the circuit,
unless you stop frequently.

Within the town of San Gimignano just walk, admire
and enjoy. Once sated, follow the road round the town
and head out westward towards Montenidoli and Racciano
to view the last main vineyard area. The route begins on
a non-asphalted road just to the left of a car park by a
police station *(carabinieri)*. Follow the road down and
over a small stream. Immediately to the left is Signano,
Panizzi is a minute or so further on to the right and just
a little past Panizzi a very long private road leads out
to Montenidoli.

Instead, continue to San Donato. There you can turn left
onto an even rougher road and twist back round to
Pietrafitta where you started, passing Canneta on the way.
Alternatively, you can take a longer but easier course continuing south to the area's border at Castel San Gimignano,
there turning left to Colle Vald'Elsa and the Florence–Siena
roads, or right towards Volterra.

Arezzo and environs

AREZZO

WINE PRODUCERS

Villa Cilnia
Loc. Montoncello, Pieve al Bagnoro
Tel: 0575 365017; fax: 0575 365639;
E, F
Once Arezzo's flagship estate, with steep, well-aspected vineyards, things have been wobbly since a buy-out in 1995. All wines barriqued. Chianti Colli Aretini normale and Riserva, Vocato (Sangiovese/Cabernet), Mecenate (Chardonnay/Sauvignon). Visit any time, 8am-8pm without booking. Book with estate

Fattoria Santa Maria di Ambra
Loc. Ambra, Bucine
Tel: 0577 996806
Owned by the Zampi family since 15th century. Largish estate. Refined but somewhat oaky wines led by Chianti cru La Bigattiera, Casamurli (Sangiovese/Malvasia Nera), Gavignano (Cabernet/Sangiovese).

Villa La Selva
Loc. Montebenichi, Bucine
Tel: 055 998203; fax: 055 998181; E, F
High investment, top class consultants for vineyards and cellars. Vast range of wines: Chianti; varietal Sangiovese, Cabernet, Chardonnay; Vin Santo;

Below Ancient coats-of-arms adorn Arezzo's Palazzo Pretorio.

This is an optional add-on, either an extended way of reaching Montepulciano or a day-trip from Siena (an hour away). There's not much wine interest but it is worth doing, as much for the scenery as for the majesty of Arezzo.

From Siena, after 20 minutes of curving through gracious, soft hills the road gets twisty and rises inexorably. There's foresting interspersed with vineyard and olive grove, and stunning views. The vines initially lie in Chianti Colli Senesi then, before reaching the crest (almost 580m), you cross into Arezzo province and Chianti Colli Aretini. A descent brings you to Monte San Savino with its castellated medieval centre. But that's the last treat as you cross the flat, dull Chiana valley. Beware: at Arezzo's entrance is a confusing junction; keep left, with the railway to your right.

Arezzo is a well-to-do town, its wealth based mainly on gold craftworks. The modern part is smart and spacious with plentiful shopping; the old town, at the peak of the hill, is a delight. Within a few steep cobbled steps you find a large Medici fortress; a medieval/Renaissance cathedral; a glorious Romanesque church; the Basilica of San Francesco, full of Piero della Francesca frescoes; Piazza Grande, with its profusion of architectural styles; and much more. There's also the remains of a Roman amphitheatre lower down.

From Arezzo you can tour the Casentino (see p30) or head for Montepulciano. The direct way is by *autostrada*, along the Chiana valley, exiting at Val di Chiana, through Bettolle to Torrita di Siena. With luck you'll see Chianina cattle, huge, white and horned. You'll also see a few vineyards.

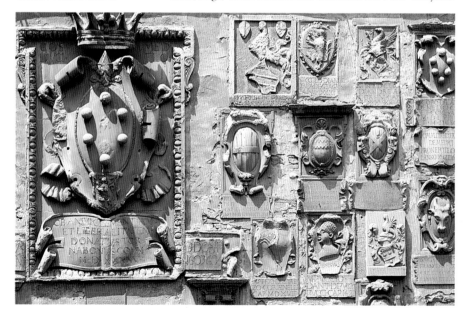

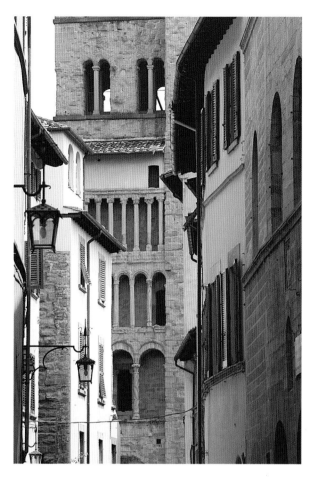

Left *The* campanile *(bell tower) of Arezzo's Santa Maria della Pieve church, half hidden behind one of its narrow, curving streets.*

sparkling wine and more. May visit without booking. Book with estate
Tenimenti Luigi d'Alessandro Manzano
Loc. Camucia, Cortona
Tel: 0575 618667; E., G, Sp.
Mid-sized estate with much investment. Intriguingly non-classic wines but of class and distinction. Podere Il Bosco (Syrah) Podere di Fontarca (Chardonnay/Viognier), Il Vescovo di Manzano (Gamay), Le Terrazze di Manzano (mainly Sauvignon). Visits mornings only. Must book.

EATING OUT

La Torre di Gnicche
Piaggia San Martino, 8
Tel: 0575 352035; eves only, cl. Wed
Simple, attractive locale in 12th century building. Carefully put together wine list, including a number of Colli Aretini wines, served by bottle or glass. Short range of traditional local dishes from fine quality ingredients. Cheese board. Inexpensive, great value.
Buca di San Francesco
Via San Francesco, 1
Tel: 0575 23271; cl. Mon eve, Tus.
Arezzo's best known and most serious restaurant. Well flavoured, classic Tuscan fare. Reasonable but rather high priced wine list.
L'Agania
Via Mazzini, 10
Tel: 0575 295381; cl. Mon
Traditional, rough and ready but friendly trattoria. Large portions. Drink house. Good value.

FOOD SHOPPING

Pane e Salute,
Corso Italia, 11
Huge range of delicious breads
Macelleria Gastronomia Aligi Barelli
Via della Chimera, 20
Salumi, ready-to-cook meat dishes, excellent Chianina beef.
Torrefazione Artigiana Donatello,
Via Vittorio Veneto, 129
Both for top notch coffees

SPECIAL EVENTS

Antiques Fair,
Piazza Vasari
First Sunday of month

The first few lie in Chianti Colli Aretini; most are for Valdichiana. For a picturesque amble, take the longer route through medieval Castiglion Fiorentino with its myriad churches. It's more viney but has views over the Chiana valley, especially from Cortona, propped on a mountain ridge, with tiny, twisting streets. Cortona is also medieval but has many Etruscan remnants. You then skirt the peaceful Lake Trasimeno (in Umbria) before turning right to Bettolle.

CHIANTI COLLI ARETINI

Sadly a low spot. Vineyards are sparse, often in poor condition and few producers make much of worth. But with the recent emergence of a few good estates, the future looks encouraging. The most promising part is on the Upper Arno's left bank, around Bucine, Mercatale and Montevarchi.

VALDICHIANA

Mainly Trebbiano with a little Malvasia, produced in the low hills of the Chiana valley. Often a light but uninspiring white, though a few producers make elegant, creamy, almondy wine.

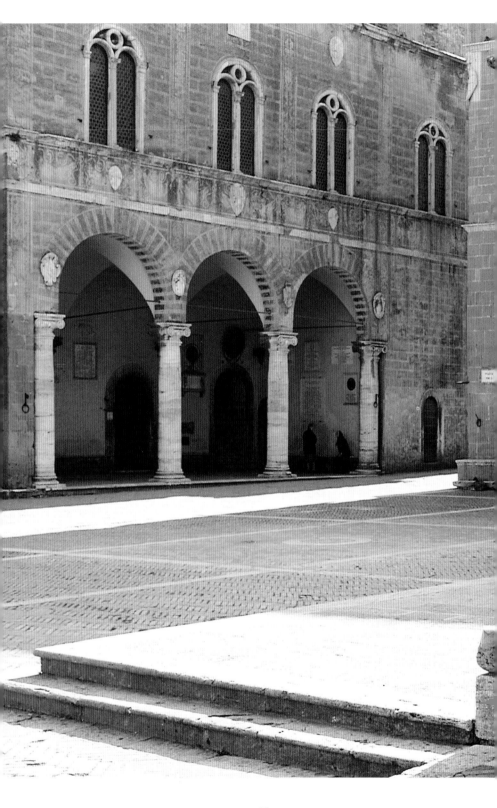

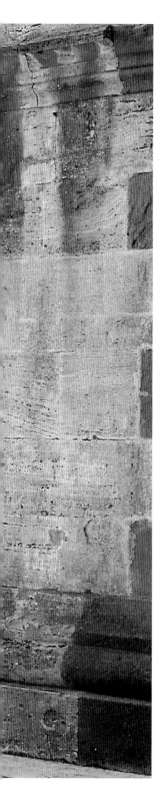

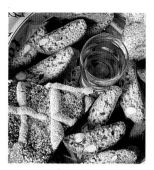

Montepulciano

Montepulciano, at just over 600 metres, is one of south-ern Tuscany's two major hill-top wine towns. It is exhil-arating to stand high and cool, staring for miles cross-country (San Quirico, over 15 kilometres away, is easily visible). It is also startling to think that as you plough up and down the steep, narrow streets you are actually walking on a network of holes: the tufaceous soil under the town has been repeatedly burrowed into over the years, from the Etruscans onwards. Uniquely, a few of the caverns are still used as cellars, just as they have been for centuries. It is salutary to imagine the amount of effort involved in hauling barrels of fresh wine up the long inclines from the vineyards below to store them in the undisturbed, constant cool of the cellars; only to send them back down again once sold. Few who have the luxury of such premises use them as their everyday working cellars any more – it's just too labour intensive, and modern-day thinking requires wines to be moved as little as possible. Some are open for visits though; opening times are posted on the doors.

GETTING THERE

You may come in to Montepulciano from Arezzo (see p78), or from Siena, along the Perugia road. Along the way you start to see deep grey fissures in the clay rock. These are known as *le crete di Siena*, a notable landmark. Most of the vineyards you pass are Chianti Colli Senesi: the signposting leaves you in no doubt. From Siena, after about half an hour you pass the major estate of Farnetella, clearly signposted. A couple of minutes further along, fork right off the main road to Sinalunga, a small, functional town of no great interest, and within ten minutes you're at Torrita di Siena. Another couple of minutes brings you into the commune of Montepulciano, where the wine zone starts too.

Left *Wandering up and down the narrow streets of Montepulciano it is startling to think that you are* *walking above networks of tunnels.* Above Crostata *partners sweet* Vin Santo *as well as* cantucci.

THE WINES

Montepulciano produces two wines, both from a blend dominated by Sangiovese (locally known as Prugnolo since the particular clone of the grape supposedly gives a plummy flavour) with Canaiolo, sometimes Mammolo, and, optionally, small quantities of the white grapes Trebbiano and Malvasia. The flagship is Vino Nobile di Montepulciano, DOCG, aged for a minimum of two years (three for the Riserva). There is quite a difference in styles between producers. Some prefer more elegant, refined wines: 'wine for the nobles'; others prefer intense, slow-ageing blockbusters: 'noble wines'. Either way, from very shaky beginnings when the wines became DOCG 15 years ago, there have been massive improvements. Now, replacing a communal chip on the shoulder is a buzz of confidence and sense of direction. Part of the reason for the upsurge in consistency of quality in Vino Nobile was the introduction of the second wine, the DOC Rosso di Montepulciano. Not only did it satisfy the need for a more youthful, fruitier style, but it helped ensure that only the best grapes went into Vino Nobile.

The soil in Montepulciano is generally loamy; a good mixture of clay, limestone and sand, interspersed with marine deposits from old tributaries of the Chiana.

Some producers also make Chianti Colli Senesi, and those with vineyards in the extreme east of the zone may also produce Valdichiana.

THE VINEYARDS

As you start to rise into Montepulciano you are surrounded by three of the area's best sub-zones; Ascianello to the right, Abbadia to the left and Gracciano ahead. Continue towards Gracciano. This is the starting point for the tour which is in two stages, two large loops, each taking a good hour.

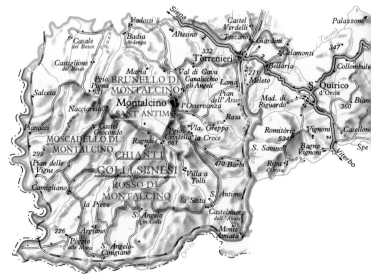

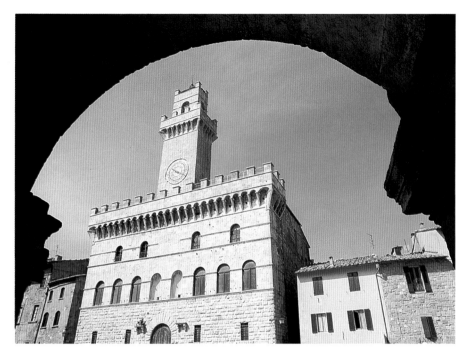

Above *The dominating Palazzo Communale in Montepulciano.*

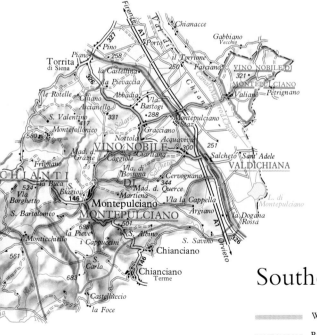

Southern Tuscany

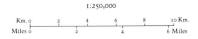 Wine route

·—·—·—· Regional boundary

·—·—·—· Provincia boundary

BRUNELLO DI
MONTALCINO **DOC/DOCG**

DOC/DOCG boundaries are distinguished
by coloured lines.

1:250,000

Km. 0   2   4   6   8   10 Km.
Miles 0   2   4   6 Miles

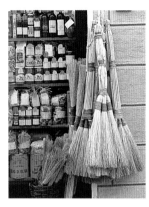

Above *Small shops still play a major role in Italian towns.*
Right *Colourful banners in Montepulciano.*
Far right *A powerful view of the town from its surroundings.*

CHIANTI COLLI SENESI

RECOMMENDED PRODUCERS

Castello di Farnetella
Sinalunga
Tel: 0576 663520
Run by Giuseppe Mazzocolin who also controls the magnificent Felsina in Chianti Classico (see p66-7), aided by consultant winemaker Franco Bernabei. Terrific Chianti Colli Senesi and classy international varietals.

Fattoria del Colle
Trequanda
Tel: 0577 662108; fax:: 0577 662202; E, G
Recently taken over by Donatella Cinelli who is working frentically to build up the wines' quality. Already cheerfully drinkable Chianti and rounded Leone Rosso (Sangiovese/Merlot). Ancient buildings with chapel, hermitage, monumental halls. Wine made in Montalcino. No need to book except for Sundays or vineyard visits. May pay for tastings. Book with estate or via agency; min stay one night.

MONTEPULCIANO

WINE PRODUCERS

All those listed below produce both Vino Nobile di Montepulciano and Rosso di Montepulciano.

Avignonesi
Tel: 0578 757872; E, F, G
Estates at Le Cappezzine, Poggetti and La Selva. Enormous, powerful, mouth-fillers of intensity, weight, extract and

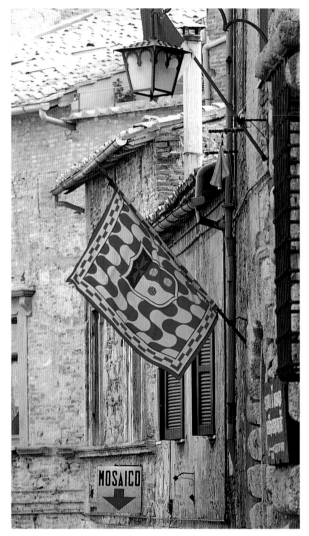

NORTHEAST MONTEPULCIANO

At Gracciano, turn left towards Valiano, passing, in quick succession, the estates Raspanti (to the left), the 18th-century Tenuta di Gracciano (left), with next door Fattoria di Gracciano followed by Fattoria di Mazzuchelli. The next modern building to the right is Poliziano. From here you descend to 250 metres, below which Montepulciano wines may not be produced, and suddenly the vineyards all but disappear. The few you see are for Valdichiana. There are remnants of *la fila*, the 18th-century system of looping vines along field boundaries. Now follow the road to the right and across the broad Chiana valley to Valiano, a separate Montepulciano sub-zone.

To the right is Lodera Nuova, followed by Tenute Trerose, a huge modern estate. You are in a small spur of

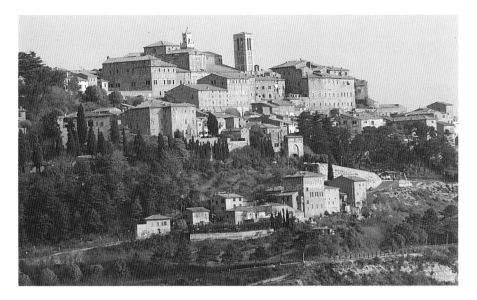

Montepulciano between the province of Arezzo (left) and the border of Tuscany with Umbria. Up ahead, slightly to the right, is the Fattoria delle Capezzine, one of three estates belonging to the Avignonesi and incorporating their barrique cellar plus another storing their much-lauded Vin Santo.

Continuing to Le Capezzine, La Calonica is just visible over a hillock to the far right. By the next small junction you are at the far extreme of Montepulciano, 15 minutes of fast driving from Gracciano. Either turn back or take a sharp right and loop back onto this road behind Trerose.

At the three-way junction just past the second railway line, fork slightly left (signposted Montepulciano). This goes behind Poliziano (right) and Nottola (right). At the next junction bend right (direction Sinalunga) and within seconds you are back at Gracciano. Now turn sharp left, signposted Fassati, and in one minute Fassati's cellars appear on the left and their vineyards on the right, with Montefollonico high up. Go on and the Salarco stream flows parallel on the right. The vineyards are Le Caggiole's, growing white grapes on the flatter land and red above, while to the right are those of Innocenti. All these are within a couple of kilometres, before the next junction. Ahead and to the left are the lands of Contucci, while round the corner is the Asinone vineyard, a special *cru* of Poliziano.

At the next T-junction go right back on to the main road. At the next junction, slip left by the Consorzio Agrario then immediately right into Via dei Canneti. This takes you under Montepulciano. Follow round (keeping the town on the left). You pass the Canneto estate and then emerge beside the San

class which take years to mature. Large range of wines; some from traditional, some from international grape varieties.

Terre di Bindella
Tel: 0578 767777; E,G
Swiss-owned. Very densely planted vineyards. High-tech cellar. Deep, concentrated wines. Visits only working hours, Mon-Fri. Pay for tastings.

Poderi Boscarelli
Tel: 0578 767277; E, F
Family-run by the lively Paola De Ferrari and sons; most welcoming. Smallish, well sited, excellently exposed vineyards yield Sangiovese of the highest quality. Some of the zone's classiest and most exciting wines, rich, weighty but refined.

La Calonica
Tel: 0578 724119; E, F
Mid-sized, at northeast limit of zone, near Lake Trasimeno, which creates its own microclimate, tempering winter cold and summer heat, and assisting humidity. Well mtyped, mid-weight wines. Pay for tastings.

Canneto
Tel: 0578 757737; E
Swiss-owned. Smallish, wines produced

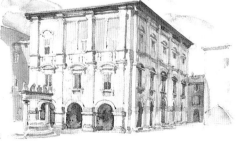

with great care and commitment to quality. Well fruited, balanced wines, in continuous improvement. Must book.

Fattoria Le Casalte
Tel: 0578 799138
Gem of an estate, run with dedication by young Chiara Barioffi. Passionate care in the vineyards: among Tuscany's

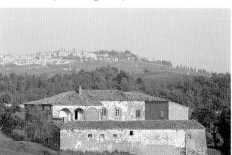

best and winemaking now rising to similar levels. Beautifully honed, well structured, elegant wines.

Dei
Tel: 0578 716878; fax: 0578 758680; E
Newish estate, run with dynamism by Caterina Dei. Prime exponent of fruitier, more elegant Vino Nobile. Must book, also for vineyard visits (spread over four areas). Pay for tastings B Due for 2000. Book with estate.

Fattoria del Cerro
Tel: 0578 767722
Large, impressive estate with over 150ha of vineyard and much additional new planting. In the forefront of viticultural experimentation. Broad portfolio of wines. Reds rich, fruity, with good body.

Fassati
Tel: 0578 708708
Large company with huge, well ordered cellars. Wines have improved greatly in recent years; now rich, full and fleshy.

Tenuta di Gracciano
Tel: 0578 708340
Small estate with excellently sited vineyards. Richly fruited, well balanced, stylish wines.

Poliziano
Tel: 0578 738171; E
Energy-bomb owner Federico Carletti is regarded as the fount of Montepulciano expertise, and the wines bear witness. Vineyards on three

Biagio church. Turn right. For views of both church and town, turn right again and go for about one kilometre, past Cantina Santavenere. Otherwise turn left, until you have come full circle, back to the Consorzio Agrario. Now, at last, you can go up to the town, park, and, on foot, experience its fascination.

EAST MONTEPULCIANO

Leave Montepulciano along the road to Chianciano Terme. Follow it until it U-bends to the right. Here go straight ahead on a minor road towards Argiano. This is the heart of Montepulciano. Passing woods on the left you see Fattoria di Paterno, then a large stretch of vineyard belonging to Fattoria del Cerro. Notice the difference between the older plots with fewer vines and the new plots which, for higher quality, have greater vine density. Fattoria del Cerro's cellars are the low, pink, dark-roofed buildings on the left. Off to the right is Le Casalte with Montepulciano's best-kept vineyards. The next stage is probably the most unspoilt part, with old cultivation systems still in evidence. Keep curving down (ignore the left fork to Argiano itself) until you leave the cultivation zone, crossing under the motorway

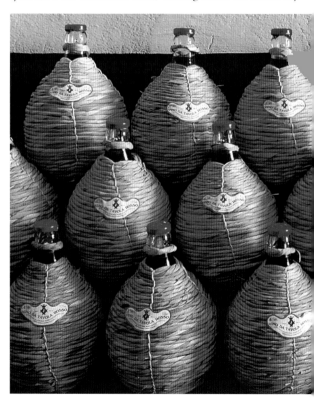

Above *Old casa colonica.*
Right *Flagons such as these have almost disappeared from Tuscany's wine zones.*
Far right *An ancient olive tree.*

and turning left onto the main road. On the left is a cypress-lined avenue to Poggio alla Sala. (This stretch takes 15–25 minutes.) Now take the main road for five minutes and just after crossing the motorway you reach Acquaviva. In the middle of the village turn left into a narrow street, towards Cervognano and wine country reappears.

An avenue on the right leads to the fine-quality, pretty estate of Poderi Boscarelli. A couple of minutes later you pass the hamlet of Cervognano and, three or four minutes after that, the estate Fanetti (right). At the junction that quickly follows either detour left to see the vineyards of Dei, or continue rightish. Seconds later, U-curve to the right onto a gem of a non-asphalted road, the Strada di Bossona. (On some maps, the road erroneously appears to stop at Bossona.) The next batch of vineyard on the right is the German-owned Il Conventino. The road descends to a crossroads, the area of Tenuta Valdipiatta. Ahead are a few shacks, so turn right, onto a rutted track until a T-junction, where you turn left, back onto asphalted road. At the next junction (with road signs) you are close to Cracciano and have completed the circuit. To return to Montepulciano, turn left.

sites. Carletti pre-selects for Rosso/Vino Nobile by plot and cultivates accordingly, rather than discriminating by grape quality, as do most. Long-lived, intense, powerful, complex wines.

Tenute Trerose
Tel: 0578 724018
Large modernistic estate. Increasingly well-made, firm wines.

Tenuta Valdipiatta
Tel: 0578 757930
Small, family-run estate. Wines of personality, style and elegance.

Agricola Romeo
Tel: 0578 757127.
Tiny estate. Wines produced with

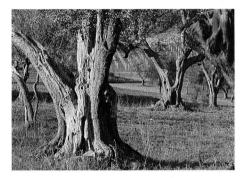

abundant care and attention: classically styled, well-balanced, with good structure and ample fruit. Must book

Salcheto
Tel: 0578 799031; E, F
Husband and wife team, completely dedicated to maximizing their vineyards' potential. Fine, fruit-forward but well-structured wines combining drinkability with longevity. An estate to watch. Book.

Tenuta S. Agnese
Tel & fax: 0578 716716; E, G
Highly traditionalist estate, one of the few still using white grapes in Vino Nobile. Must book 3 months prior.

HOTELS

Locanda dell'Amoroso
Tel: 0577 679497; fax: 0577 632001
Wonderful, relaxing spot in 14th-century hamlet. Pretty rooms, all different, excellent bathrooms. Parking.

La Chiusa
Tel: 0577 669668; fax: 0577 669593
Small, with a personal touch. Rooms simply but tastefully furnished, good bathrooms. Parking.

Hotel Residence Casanova
San Quirico
Tel: 0577 898177; fax: 0577 898190
Spacious, refined, restful. In typical Tuscan style but with all mod cons. Swimming pool.

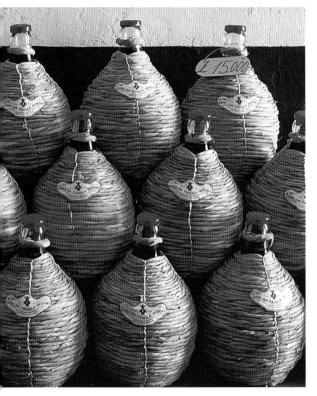

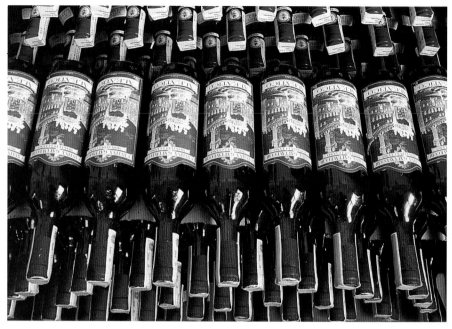

Above *Newly bottled wine awaits release for sale.*
Right and below right *The vine-dominated landscape around Montepulciano and Montalcino.*
Centre *'Poliziano' was the ancient name for Montepulciano.*
Far right *Wooden stakes, used to support the wires in the vineyard.*

EATING OUT

Locanda dell'Amorosa
Loc. L'Amorosa, Sinalunga
Tel: 0577 679497; cl. Tue lunch, Mon
Relaxing restaurant with fine, elegant, inviting dishes. Wide-ranging wine list. Seats outside. Fairly costly. Wine bar attached. Food products on sale. Also hotel (see below).

La Chiusa
Montefollonico
Tel: 0577 669668; cl. Tue
Tranquil, smart, top-notch place but expensive, especially the wines (mainly local). Refined dishes rooted in Tuscan traditions. Seats outside. Also hotel (see below).

Diva e Maceo
Via di Gracciano nel Corso, 90/92
Tel: 0578 716951; cl. Tue
Staunchly traditional dishes from local ingredients, served with care. Good wine list, also locally based. Good value.

Tiziana
SS326, 156
Tel: 0578 767760; cl. Mon (winter only)
Unexciting surroundings but good

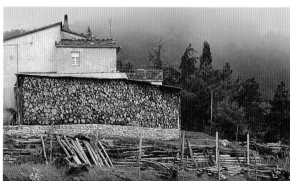

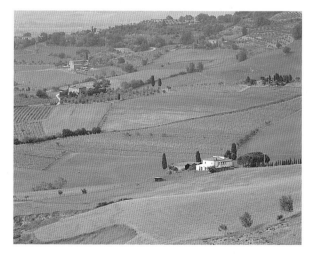

MONTEPULCIANO TO MONTALCINO

The drive between Montepulciano and Montalcino is not only one of Tuscany's most beautiful but shows strikingly how land use follows the natural contours of the terrain.

From Montepulciano, head along the Orcia valley towards Pienza, keeping an eye out behind where there is a series of majestic views of the town dominating the landscape. Even after leaving the wine zone (contiguous with the commune) vines linger, producing Chianti Colli Senesi. This attractive stretch of rolling hills brings much more mixed cultivation, with numerous fruit and vegetable plots, and grazing areas for sheep. Then, lower down, grain cultivation takes over.

Within 15 minutes you reach Pienza, a Renaissance town, one of the first experiments in town planning and designed to be pleasing and restful to the eye. The main piazza, with its decorated alcoves, is a delight that slows even harassed visitors to a lingering crawl. There is more tranquillity just outside in the Romanesque Pieve di Corsignano. Pienza is renowned for its sheep's cheeses: ricotta and the locally famous Pecorino di Pienza; and a speciality biscuit named after Lucrezia Borgia.

From the rise at Pienza there's a further descent into a huge, exhilarating stretch of open countryside, rather like a gigantic saucer with its rim a far ring of hills. Then the land rises once more, as the small, smart town of San Quirico approaches. San Quirico leads to Bagno Vignoni, a popular spa resort where hot springs continually gush out at 40°C. Some of the pools are even open all night on summer weekends.

However, for Montalcino, skirt the town, in the direction of Siena. Soon the scenery becomes barer and more rugged, the first signs of the famous 'moonscape' that dominates much of southwestern Tuscany late in the year when expanses of blue-grey clay give a weirdly evocative, unworldly effect. Once at Torrenieri, Montalcino is signposted, vineyards begin once more then, suddenly, the town appears, just under 600 metres high astride a huge massif – a surprisingly awe-inspiring sight.

Tuscan food based on fine ingredients and skilled cooking. Well chosen wines. Inexpensive, good value.

La Grotta
Loc. San Biagio, 15
Tel: 0578 757607; cl. Wed
Opposite San Biagio church. Tuscan classics but with individuality and refinement. Large, wide-ranging wine list. Seats outside.

Latte di Luna
Pienza, Via San Carlo, 2/4
Tel: 0578 748606; cl. Tue
Delightful, welcoming trattoria serving Tuscan classics with care and attention. Small but good wine list. Seats outside. Good value.

Osteria del Leone
Loc. Bagno Vignoni, San Quirico
Tel: 0577 887300; cl. Mon
Lively, friendly trattoria; Tuscan classics cooked to perfection. Wide range of wines. Seats outside. Good value.

Antico Caffè Poliziano
Very elegant bar, established 1868. Good coffee, snacks. Extensive views.

PLACES OF INTEREST

Cantina dei Redi
Recently rediscovered; the best of the underground cellars. Probably Etruscan, now mostly 14th-15th century. Some parts of vast height, others cavernously low. Also shop with wines, foods, ceramics. Ring number on door if closed.

ENOTECHE

Borgo Buio
New and Montepulciano's brightest star. Fine range of wines, good snacks, tutored tastings.

Oinochoé
Large, countrywide selection.

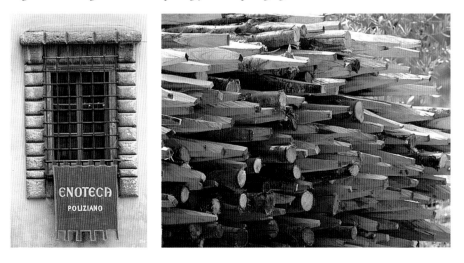

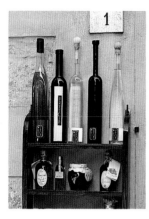

FOOD SHOPPING

Silvana Cugusi
Good cheeses, especially Pecorino di Pienza.
Salumeria Augusto Binarelli

PIENZA AND SAN QUIRICO

HOTELS

Hotel Residence Casanova
San Quirico
Tel: 0577 898177
A haven. Spacious, refined, restful, designed in typical Tuscan style but all mod cons. Swimming pool.
Hotel Posta
Bagno Vignoni Tel: 0577 887112
Steaming natural swimming pool: bubbling hot water (40°C).

RESTAURANTS

La Buca delle Fate
Pienza Tel: 0578 748448
Long bench tables, homely cooking. Classic Tuscan dishes. Montepulciano wines in carafe, also by the glass at the bar. Closed Mondays.
Taverna di Moranda
Monticchello (Pienza)
Tel: 0578 755050
Smart but inexpensive traditional fare. Great local wine list. Closed Mondays.
Osteria del Leone
Bagno Vignoni, San Quirico
Tel: 0577 887300
Tasty, substantial dishes, traditional. Good local wine list. Not costly. Cl Mon.

MONTALCINO

WINE PRODUCERS

Unless stated otherwise, all those listed below produce Brunello di Montalcino and Rosso di Montalcino. 'Brunello' on

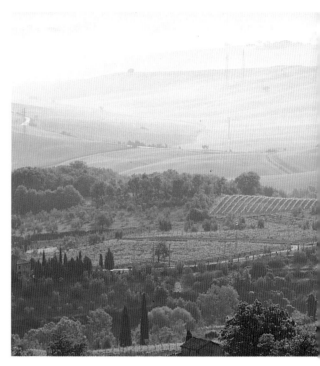

Montalcino

Wine seems to ooze from the pores of Montalcino. There are seemingly far too many *enoteche* for such a small place; restaurants and *trattorie* all have a plentiful selection of bottles; even humble bars boast dozens of labels. The square beneath the vast fortress overlooking the town emphasizes the point by a giant plaque, courtesy of the Brunello di Montalcino Consorzio, indicating its estates.

Yet Montalcino's wine history is relatively recent. Although produced here for centuries, it is only in the past 130 years that its wines have become such a talking-point, whereas Montepulciano's proximity to trade routes brought it to attention sooner. The much-repeated story of Montalcino's rise to fame is that the Biondi-Santi family created the wine's style and quality by propagating the Brunello grape (a particular Sangiovese clone) and by using it unblended. However, several luminaries dispute this with strong evidence. Whatever the truth, no other area in Italy has sustained such consistently high quality for such a high proportion of its wines.

GETTING THERE

Montalcino is just half an hour from Montepulciano and less than an hour from Siena. A fair bit of the route from Siena involves the slow Via Cassia but, gradually, by-passes and dual-carriageway stretches are being built to ease congestion. The road follows the Arbia valley and fog can sometimes be

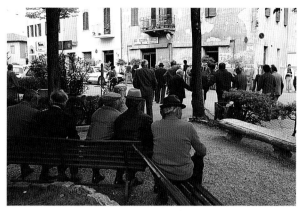

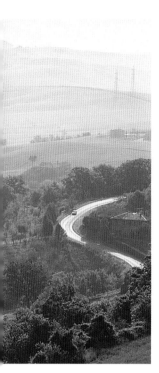

Above *Pienza was developed in the Renaissance and was one of the first experiments in town planning.* Left *Grappa, Italy's equivalent of the French brandy marc, is made from the skins and pips of grapes from which wine has been made.*

a hazard. These lands are fertile and grow cereals and fruits alongside grazing for sheep and Chianina cattle. It is a comparatively boring stretch so it is a relief to reach Buoncenvento, where the Arbia flows into the Ombrone, south Tuscany's most important river. Just past the town Montalcino is first signposted. Within a minute or two you enter the wine zone. The road curves and suddenly, Montalcino astride its hill is in view, a breathtaking sight. The scenery as you rise is stupendous – photographs never do justice to its softly coloured, often misty, wide expanses.

THE WINES

Montalcino's reputation hangs on Brunello di Montalcino (DOCG), made exclusively from the Brunello grape, a particular Sangiovese clone. It is aged four or more years before sale, with at least the first two in wood and at least the last few months in bottle. It is slow-maturing and long-lived, giving big, richly fruited, powerful, intensely flavoured, complex red wines. If proof were needed that Sangiovese is capable of producing some of the world's top wines, Brunello di Montalcino would be it. Nearly all producers also make Rosso di Montalcino (DOC), also exclusively from Brunello: it is younger (one year's minimum ageing), livelier, less intense and more overtly fruity, yet still stylish and fairly concentrated.

In recent years there has also been a revival of Moscadello di Montalcino. The white Moscadello grape (similar to Moscato Bianco) produces light, fresh and refreshing, won-

its own refers to the grape.

Altesino
Tel: 0577 806208; E, G, Dan
Textbook cellars, smart and spotless. Elegant, supple, fruit-forward wines. Also Rosso di Artesino (95% Brunello), Arte d'Altesi (70% Brunello), both with Cabernet Sauvignon; Palazzo d'Altesi (Brunello); Borgo d'Altesi (Cabernet); Quarto d'Altesi (Brunello/ Merlot/Cabernet). Groups pay for tastings, and should pre-book.

Tenuta di Argiano
Tel: 0577 864037
The most imposing villa in Montalcino in one of its most imposing positions. Broad, powerful wines of personality.

Banfi
Tel: 0577 840111; fax: 0577 840205 E, F, G
Conceived by the massive Banfi corporation, huge American importers of Italian wine, and spearheaded the revival of Moscadello. Over 800ha of vineyards of which 150ha produce Brunello di Montalcino, and one of Italy's largest cellars, a stainless steel palace linked to a palace of oak. Vast number of wines produced, from international varieties as well as Brunello or Brunello blends. These shine for textbook typicity of style rather than individuality. Pay for tastings. Must book with estate 6 months prior.

Fattoria dei Barbi
Tel: 0577 848277
High-profile estate run with panache by Francesca Colombini Cinelli. Wine quality in steady improvement. Riserva Vigna del Fiore leads smallish range, firmly based on Brunello. On-site meals and snacks available at La Taverna dei Barbi (not Wed).

Biondi-Santi
Tel: 0577 847121; E, F
High reputation, high prices and, finally, after a few years in the

doldrums, high quality again. Classy, slow-aging wines. Also Sassoalloro (Brunello), Schidione (Brunello/ Cabernet/Merlot), Lavischio (Merlot), Moscadello, Rivolo (Sauvignon).

Casanova di Neri
Tel: 0577 834029
Smallish estate. Wines, strongly characterful, concentrated and of firm attack, produced with assiduous care both in vineyard and cellar.

Casato Prime Donne
Tel: 0577 849421; E, F
'Feminist' estate run by Donatello Cinelli Colombini (daughter of Barbi's Francesca) with a mainly female team. Brunello di Montalcino 'Progetto

derfully grapey and gently sweet wines. There are three styles: still, *frizzante* (slightly sparkling) and *vendemmia tardiva* (late harvest). This last, made from grapes picked later than normal to increase ripeness and then sometimes left to dry a short while to concentrate them further, is stronger and fuller flavoured. Producers differ as to which type represents the 'true' Moscadello and rarely make more than one style.

There is also one other DOC, the newish Sant'Antino, from vineyards near the eponymous church in the southern part of Montalcino. It is a tiny zone making a large number of wines: single-varietal Cabernet Sauvignon, Merlot, Pinot Nero, Chardonnay, Sauvignon and Pinot Grigio; a red blend, a white blend, plus two types of Vin Santo.

THE VINEYARDS

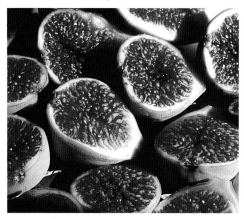

Montalcino's vineyard area is bounded by three rivers: the Orcia, Asso and Ombrone. It also divides naturally into three sub-zones. Vineyards to the north tend to produce lighter, more elegant wines; those to the east, sheltered from the prevailing weather systems, are more structured and firmer while those to the warmer south, where the Mediterranean exerts a gently moderating influence, make the biggest, richest, most powerful wines There are a few estates to the northwest too. It is logical to see them in these three groupings.

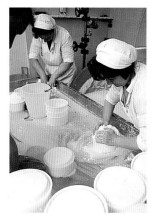

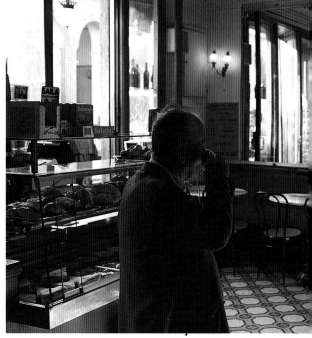

Top *Tuscan meals often finish off simply with fresh seasonal fruit such as figs.*
Above *Workers busily produce Pecorino cheese at Fattoria dei Barbi.*
Right *La Fiaschetteria, the meeting place in Montalcino, with a fantastic cellar of wines.*

NORTH MONTALCINO

Estates are closely clustered in the north and can be seen in a little over half an hour. Nearly all roads out of Montalcino leave from just under the Fortezza at the south end of town, but you need to leave from the north, through the Porta Burelli. From here, there's a steep descent on a heavenly, non-asphalted road, initially walled, then opening out. Go through the gate-posts ahead then turn right at the next T-junction. This leads onto the hill of Montosoli, with vineyards belonging to Altesino and others. You pass those of Capanna di Cencione then, after a left-hand curve, a pair of cypresses on the hill to the left marks 'La Casa', a cru of Tenuta di Caparzo.

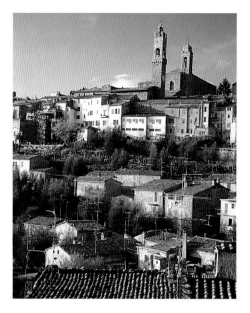

After a large bend to the right, the Valdicava estate appears (right). Seconds later, turn left and right in quick succession (call this spot Point A) and all signs of vine cultivation vanish. Two minutes further on you pass the signpost for Torrenieri (Montalcino's threshold and the site of Casanova di Neri). Keep going straight until a fork where you left (the white house visible leftwards is Altesino). You pass Tenuta di Caparzo along a cypress-lined lane, followed by Altesino.

Another big leftward curve and you are almost at the zone's edge with the Via Cassia in sight. Turn left at the 'Stop' sign,

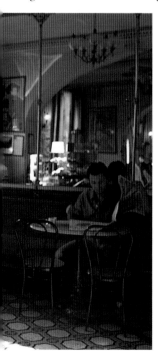

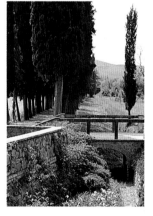

Top *Sun shines on Montalcino town, which is packed with enoteche, bars and restaurants offering good ranges of wines.* Above *Cypresses lead up to Tenuta Col d'Orcia.*

Prime Donne' produced with the guidance of four female experts (including this guide's author). Wine artefacts in cellars. Book for weekend visits. May pay for tastings.

Castelgiocondo
Tel: 055 27141; E, F, G
Large, owned by Frescobaldi (Chianti Rufina). Wines vary strongly with vintage. Also Lamaione (Merlot), Vergena (Sauvignon). Frescobaldi are also involved in a joint venture with California's Mondavi company to produce Luce (Brunello/Merlot) nearby.

Cerbaiona
Tel: 0577 848660
Jewel of an estate; small, family-run with, in good vintages, superb, full, supple but well structured wines that 'sing'. Also Cerbaiona Rosso (Brunello).

Col d'Orcia
Tel: 0577 808001; E, F, G
Stylish, fine, well-balanced wines. Also Olmaia (Merlot), Le Ghiaie (Chardonnay), Moscadello, others. Ask for vineyard visits.

Costanti
Tel: 0577 848195; E, F, G
Smallish, with lovingly tended vineyards. Firm, elegant and beautifully honed, classy wines. Also Vermiglio (Brunello), Ardingo (Merlot/Cabernet). Must book.

Eredi Fuligni
Tel: 0577 848127; E, F, G
Rising star. Complex, rich wines of individuality. Must book.

La Fortuna
Tel: 0577 848308

Tiny, friendly estate with ever-improving, fruit-forward, moreish wines.

Lisini
Tel: 0577 864040
Lean, firmly structured wines that need a bit of coaxing to show their character. But once they do, the refinement, fruit and enlivening spiciness make the wait worthwhile.

Mocali
Tel: 0577 849485; E
Very small estate, perfectly sited: in west of zone, comparatively cool, well exposed and well aerated. Firm, powerful, classically styled wines. Also I Piaggioni (Brunello).

Tenute Silvio Nardi
Tel: 0577 808332; E, F
Out at the extreme northwest corner of the zone. A recent change in direction has resulted in vastly improved wines, well structured and vibrant. Also Chianti, Vin Santo. Pay for visits, which include tasting and snack. Must book.

Pieve Santa Restituta
Fax: 0173 635256; E
Owned by the mythical Angelo Gaja from Piedmont. Two crus of Brunello di Montalcino plus Promis (Brunello). No tastings (try wines in the town's enoteche). Send requests for visits by fax, with good warning.

Il Poggione
Tel: 0577 844029
The essence of Montalcino. Large, powerful, complex, long-lasting wines that can thrill and enthral. Very careful selection of grapes ensures super-high quality, whatever the vintage. Winemaker Fabrizio Bindocci is fearsomely jealous of Il Poggione's reputation, the best way to ensure its perpetuation. Don't leave the area without trying some. Also Moscadello and others. Must book.

Above *Castello Banfi, now owned by huge American corporation Banfi.*
Below *Montalcino's vineyards have increased greatly in the last 20 years.*

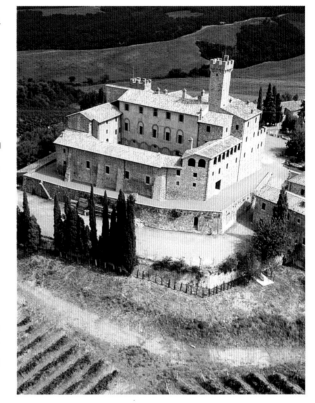

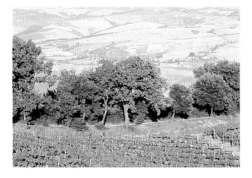

and head back up southwards. Shortly you are back at Point A (see above). Continue climbing into Montalcino heartland. The scenery around here is dominated by the Val di Suga estate. Once past its flag-bedecked buildings and immaculate vineyards, take the next right onto a narrow, steep, unmade road, the Canalicchio. It marks another area densely populated with estates: Canalicchio di Sotto, Canalicchio di Sopra, La Gerla and others. In a cloud of dust the road levels out and you are back at the beginning of the circuit.

EAST MONTALCINO

The eastern estates are even more densely packed than those to the north and can be seen in about 20 minutes. This time leave the town from under the fortress. Take the leftmost of the roads in front (direction Siena) and head downhill. Follow the road until the first junction beyond the large left-hand curve, and there fork right. Costanti is on the right with Greppone Mazzi behind and (in clear weather) the hulking mass of Monte Amiata on the horizon.

Fork right again, onto an unmade road, through a group of tiny estates, Fornacella,

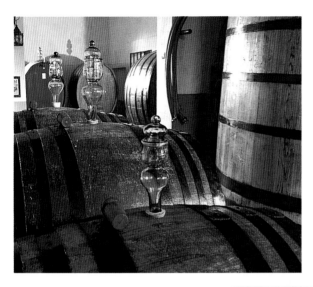

Poggio Antico
Tel: 0577 848044; E, F
Large estate with well exposed and well tended vineyard. Restrained, elegant wines of good style. Also Altero (Brunello). Must book.

Tenuta Valdicava
Tel: 0577 848261
Soft, rounded wines with concentrated fruit flavours and good breadth, from fully ripe grapes.

Val di Suga
Tel: 0577 848701
Large, modern estate. Wines of high quality, classically typed, with good

Fornacina and La Fornace (doubtless once the site of a major furnace). From there keep left and drive for a couple of minutes along a pretty, peaceful road with good views: the towers of San Quirico and Pienza rise in the distance. Practically the last house you come to is San Filippo, an attractive place surrounded by its own vineyards, before the road comes to an end. Turn back on yourself and at the second junction (with signposts to numerous estates) swing round to the right onto another pretty road, running

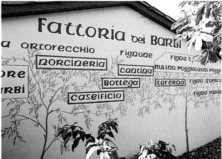

under the town. Within a couple of minutes you leave east Montalcino, marked by the Canalicchio track (with a clump of signs) to the left. Take this to get back up to town.

fruit and firm structure.

HOTELS

Bellaria
Via Osticcio, 19
Tel: 0577 849326; fax: 0577 848668
New but in traditional style, simple and comfortable. Garden. parking. 3*.

Dei Capitani
Via Lapini, 6
Tel & fax: 0577 847227
In refurbished period building. Cleanly furnished rooms, some with good views. Small pool. Parking. 3*.

SOUTH MONTALCINO

The estates of south Montalcino are much more widely spaced and to see the area properly takes about one and a half hours. It is, though, Montalcino's most gloriously scenic part and worth dallying over. Leave town from under the fortress, and take the middle road towards Castelnuovo dell'Abate. Three minutes on is a clump of trees to the left with a cypress avenue leading from it. This is Il Greppo, Biondi-Santi's estate. Then, past a relatively flat area, an avenue on the left leads to Fattoria dei Barbi. By now, weather permitting, there should be really good views of Mount Amiata ahead. Soon, there are the first sights of Mediterranean scrub, a sure sign that this zone is considerably warmer than any covered so far.

The next real interest spot is Sant'Antimo, a remarkable, simple, tranquil 12th-century church that apparently springs out of nowhere. Follow the road under Castelnuovo dell'Abate

EATING OUT

Sciame
Via Ricasoli, 9
Tel: 0577 848017; cl. Tue
Halfway between trattoria and restaurant, long-standing, friendly. Typical Tuscan specialities. Mid-length wine list, mostly local, well-chosen. Fairly inexpensive.

Il Pozzo
Loc. Sant'Angelo in Colle

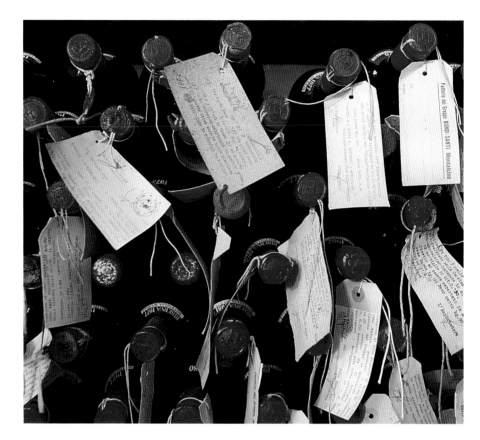

Test bottles (above) *lie maturing at Biondi Santi* (centre).
Far right (top) *The crumbling* casa colonica *near Montalcino.*
Far right (bottom) *Gleaming stainless steel vats at Tenuta Col d'Orcia.*

Tel: 0577 844015; cl. Tue
Mouthwatering, well-flavoured, wholesome Tuscan fare, especially the meat. Great olive oil; plentiful selection of local wines. Very good value.

Poggio Antico
Loc. I Poggi
Tel: 0577 849200; cl. Mon
Smart restaurant on Poggio Antico estate. Refined dishes of impeccable quality, light and flavoursome, with good service and tranquil surroundings. Extensive wine list. Surprisingly good value.

Porta al Cassero
Via della Libertà, 9
Tel: 0577 847196; cl. Wed
Wonderful old building. Go for a glass and a snack or full meals, classically Tuscan. Home made pasta. Small

through wild, forested countryside, interspersed with vineyard patches and olive trees, some very old. The village on the hill ahead is Sant'Angelo in Colle and you approach it through some of the southernmost lands of the zone.

Turn left at the next T-junction and follow the road beneath Sant'Angelo in Colle. It is worth diverting up into this peaceful village for the stunning views over southern Montalcino including the full extent of the Banfi vineyards (see below). Back down on the main road, the first estate to the right is Pian di Conte, a retirement present given by Il Poggione to their much-loved and talented winemaker, the aptly named Talenti, who sadly died late in 1999.

The next junction, *Bivio Argiano,* is named after the estate imposingly sited there. Five minutes out of Sant'Angelo in Colle you come to Sant'Angelo Scalo, a rather dull village marking Montalcino's southern boundary. There is still much more to see, so swing right and head back northwards.

The massive complex down to the left is the headquarters of Banfi. For the next 15 minutes, perfectly serried vines completely fill the landscape – so unlike anywhere else in Montalcino, where vineyard naturally meshes in with olives, forest and grain – and practically all belong to the huge Banfi territory. The left side is punctuated by the castle of Poggio alle

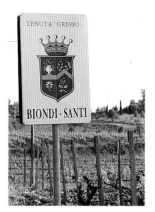

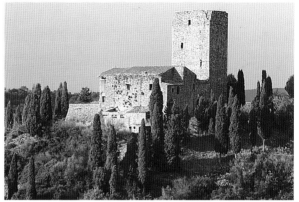

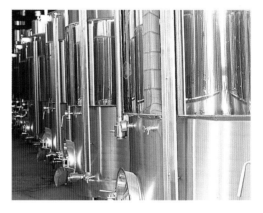

Mura, also owned by Banfi and completely (and expensively) restored by them. Apart from its use for functions, it holds an enthralling and valuable collection of antique wine bottles and glasses, which is open to the public.

A few minutes later is the hamlet of Camigliano, with the eponymous estate down to the left. At this point you feel as if you are travelling through a large vineyard saucer, rimmed by hills. The high-point of this rim is to the west (left), the hill-top town of Roccastrada, a good 20 km away. A further few minutes brings you to the edge of the village of Tavernelle. At this point a side road (left) will take you to Castelgiocondo. Just past the village another side road (to the right) leads to a series of estates. There is a great column of road signs, all facing in the other direction. Take this right turn for a five-minute diversion to Caprili, the first estate to the left, through foresting; Case Basse, literally 'two low houses' straddling the road which passes between them; and Chiesa di Santa Restituta, whose vineyards surround the ancient church.

Back on the main road the more normal mixed cultivation returns and you pass Tenuta Friggiali (left). Less than five minutes brings you to a T-junction, where you turn right. At this point Montalcino town is a mere five minutes away. Turn left at the next junction, very close by (right leads to Poggio Antico) and from there it is simply a straight climb back into town.

MONTALCINO WOODLANDS

This is a 30-minute amble, most of it through cool, dark green forest, to the sparse estates in the northwest and, optionally, back to Siena. Leave Montalcino under the fortress on the right-hand road towards Grosseto and Tavernelle. Five minutes on, at a batch of signs all pointing left (including Tavernelle), turn right, and from here merely follow the twisting lane.

selection of local wines or drink house.

ENOTECHE

Bruno Dalmazio
La Fortezza
Osticcio
Also La Fiaschetteria is the meeting place in Montalcino and Drogheria Franci has a good wine selection too.

FOOD SHOPPING

Great honey at Drogheria Franci
Local biscuits called Ossi di morti at Forno Lambardi.

PLACES OF INTEREST

La Fortezza
Tel: 0577 849211
Apart from the comprehensive collection of wines to taste, drink or buy, and accompanying light snacks, there are fabulous panoramic views from the ramparts. Eccentrically closes from 1.00-2.00pm.

SPECIAL EVENT

Honey Week, first weekend of Sept.

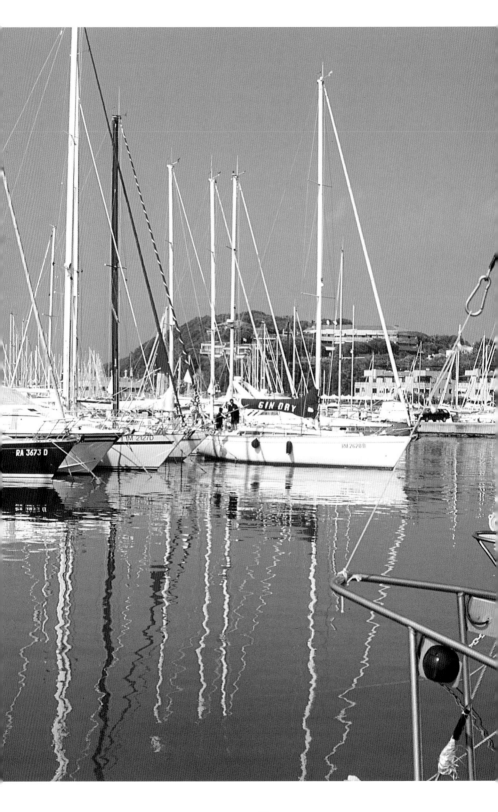

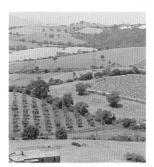

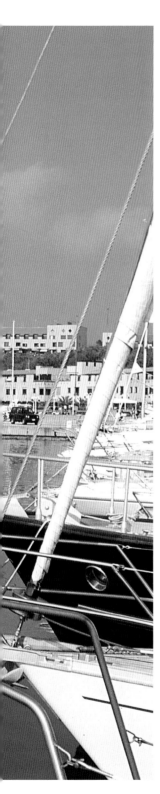

Grosseto and the Maremma

After Chianti Classico, Montepulciano and Montalcino, you may think you have seen the best of Tuscany. You have a surprise in store. There may be few other areas with as much vineyard land, but as far as natural beauty is concerned there is plenty to see, some more glorious than before. And a few sparse outcrops of vineyard can catch the spirit of viticultural endeavour even more powerfully than endless vine swaths.

There is a choice of routes to Grosseto. The longer one, looping round the southern edge of Tuscany, good for general touring but more or less vine-free, heads through Acquapendente and Lake Bolsena (reached slowly via Sant' Antonio and Mount Amiata or faster via San Quirico). The alternative, keeping the wine theme alive, is to go straight to Grosseto, in the southwest of the region, and use it as a base for exploring the southern Tuscan wine zones. Leave the Montalcino zone at Sant'Angelo Scalo, cross the river Orcia and immediately turn right. This brings you into the province of Grosseto and, in less than an hour, the town itself.

ARCIDOSSO AND MOUNT AMIATA

An optional add-on but it gives a rich taste of the diversity of the southern Tuscan countryside and reveals an emerging wine zone. After crossing the river Orcia turn left and make for Arcidosso. After a few minutes, you suddenly plunge into a wild, hilly landscape covered with Mediterranean scrub. These are the lower slopes of Mount Amiata, which soars up ahead at over 1700m. The hill-top town to the left is Montegiovi, then some outcrops of bare, blue-grey clay mark your arrival at Arcidosso. Take a large U-turn to the right at the town's entrance, towards Monticello. There follows a series of swift scenery changes until, past Monticello, the country opens out

Left *Punta Ala on the Grosseto coast. An additional bonus of Grosseto town is that it is a short* *hop through cool pine forests to the sea, with beaches at Marina di Grosseto and Principina a Mare.*

Right *Food in the Maremma generally follows Tuscan norms, with cheeses, well flavoured pasta and delicious game when in season.*

GROSSETO

EATING OUT

Lorena
Grosseto, Via Mameli, 23
Tel: 0564 22695; cl. Mon
Unusually, within a hotel. Fish- or meat-based menus, both good. Attentive service. Well matched wine list.

Il Canto del Grillo
Grosseto, Via Mazzini, 29
Tel: 0564 414589; eves only, cl. Sun
Tiny place, tucked into city walls. Food seasonal, abundant vegetables. Many non-meat dishes but succulent meats will tempt carnivores too. Good choice of local wines. Cash only.

Da Primo alla Parolaccia
Grosseto, Loc. Canonica
Tel: 0564 402205; cl. Fri
Family-run trattoria, simple and homely. Local classics cooked with aplomb. Short, decent list of local wines.

HOTELS

Nuovo Grosseto
Piazza Marconi, 26
Tel & fax: 0564 414105
Just by the station (but triple glazed). Solid, old building, completely renovated. Run with charm and professionalism. Clean and comfortable. Parking. 3*.

I Due Pini
Marina di Grosseto
Tel: 0564 34607
Run by Grosseto's leading trainer of

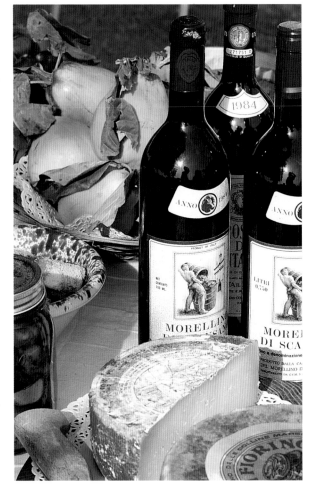

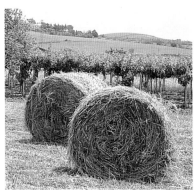

Above *Land in the Maremma is intensely cultivated, mostly with grain. Olives, the next most important crop, cluster on the hills.*

into what appears a rather rougher version of Montalcino. This is a part of the nearby DOC zone of Montecucco, lying just across the valley from Montalcino and making Sangiovese-based reds that shadow it plus Vermentino-based whites. Fifteen minutes later you cross the River Ombrone. At the next junction turn left to rejoin the Grosseto road.

GROSSETO

Grosseto is a self-assured, small, smart commercial town. It is convenient for shopping, with everything available and all within a small radius. It is also clean, well cared for and unspoilt by modern development. It was once a walled city, dominated by its Medici fortress. The ramparts of the city walls have been preserved and are now a broad, tree-shaded walkway. Each of its six bulwarks has been emphasized by a large clump of trees, making the aerial view ususually pretty. Much of the old moat has been left to grass too, although certain sections are now used as car parks. Life, as usual, centres round the main piazza, where there's the cathedral and the ornate, turreted Palazzo della Provincia.

An additional bonus is that Grosseto is just a short hop through cool pine forest to the beaches of Marina di Grosseto and Principina a Mare.

THE MAREMMA

The name Maremma most probably derives from *marittima*, land by the sea. It generally refers to Grosseto province, although its boundaries include a little territory in the adjacent province of Viterbo (in Lazio, not Tuscany). It is noticeably warmer than northern Tuscany, the light more golden, the air balmier. If you like light, open spaces, softly undulating hills cutting across azure skies, glimpses of the sea and extensive views punctuated by olive groves, you'll like the Maremma.

Although hills are never far away, there is a broadish strip of coastal plain. This is perfectly flat and was, until a massive programme of drainage in the 1930s, humid, malarial, mosquito-ravaged marshland prompting all who could to flee to the hills in summer. It is now cut through by the railway and the fast Aurelia, the SS1, the first state road (from Rome to the French border) built by Mussolini. Today's new Aurelia runs parallel in parts to the old Aurelia, which itself is a reworking of the original Roman Aurelia. The name, however, remains.

The local large, black cattle are the Maremmana breed. It is a matter of great local pride that their horns are longer than the Chianina. The area also houses one of Italy's most important natural parks, along the coast north and south of Alberese; a bird sanctuary on Orbetello and a nature reserve at Burano, both protected by the WWF. Maremma is an IGT, and is used by many of the area's vines.

sommeliers so wine plays a leading role. Homely, family-run. Garden. Near beach. 3*.

FOOD SHOPPING

All is concentrated around Via San Martino, behind Palazzo della Provincia off the main piazza. There are food shops, a gastronomia, a butcher, an enoteca and more. Leo Chiti in Via dei Barberi is another fine butcher who also sells prepared meat products.

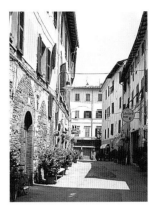

Above *Grosseto is a clean, well cared for place where modern development has not been allowed to ruin the old centre.*

Below *Maremma's coastal plain was once overrun by mosquitoe in summer and can be fiercely humid.*

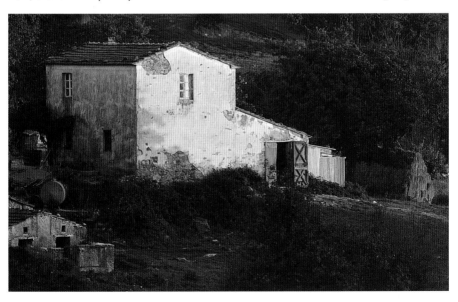

Morellino di Scansano

MORELLINO DI SCANSANO

WINE PRODUCERS

Erik Banti
Tel: 0564 508006; E, F, G, Sp, Dan
Banti, half-Danish, half-Roman, is an
exuberant Morellino protagonist.
Rounded wines of personality. Organic.
Must book. Wine accessories shop.

Bargagli
Tel: 0564 599237
Much cited by Scansano folk.

Mantellassi
Tel: 0564 592037

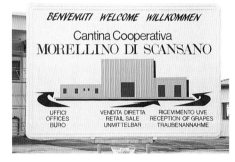

The oldest Morellino estate (since
1958). Firm, chunky, stylish wines.

Le Pupille
Tel: 0564 505129; E, F
The biggest, punchiest and, most
agree, the classiest wines of the area;
made by a couple hell bent on
pushing quality ever higher. Three
styles of Morellino, Saffredi
(Cabernet/Merlot/Alicante), Solalto
(Sauvignon/Traminer/Sémillon, sweet)

Moris Farms
Tel: 0566 619135
Scansano's rising star. Large estate,
with fine views. Rich, deep, finely-
honed wines.

Villa Patrizia
*Tel: 0564 982028; fax: 0564 982140;
Italian only*
Smallish, family run. Concentrated, full
wines. Pay for tastings. Book rooms
with estate one month prior.

EATING OUT

Antica Trattoria Aurora
Magliano, Via Chiasso Lavagnini, 12-14

Right *The Cantina Sociale di
Morellino is one of Europe's highest
cellars (at 600m).*

This is not only the most important wine of southern Tuscany but is one of the region's most talked about. It was reputedly first made by people taking refuge in Scansano's hills to escape the Maremma swamps, possibly for the Grosseto bureaucracy who decamped there. More recently, apart from a period as the 'in' wine in Florence, its star shone faintly until luminaries from leading estates in Tuscany and throughout Italy recently started to buy up vineyards and invest in its production.

THE WINE

'Morellino' is a diminutive of morello. The name could derive from the wine's colour or the breed of horses, *cavalli morelli*, that once drew the carriages of Grosseto's aristocracy. In either event, Morellino is yet another Sangiovese clone. It is used either exclusively, or with up to 15 percent of other grapes of which Alicante (known as Garnacha in Spain, Grenache in France and Cannonau in Sardinia) is the most favoured. Those who use Alicante say it is responsible for Morellino's characteristic flavour: Chianti-like but softer, lighter, rounder and more open. Others attribute the style to the area's warmer climate and lighter soil. Most pride has traditionally been invested in the Riservas which have two years' ageing, at least one of which is in cask. However, with the new wave of interest engulfing the area, the styles of both normale and Riserva are in steady evolution and much could change.

THE VINEYARDS

The area is quite extensive, forming a diamond shape from just east of Grosseto eastwards to the Saturnia spa, and equivalent distances north south. Within, there are some sensational stretches. The best approach is from the south. From

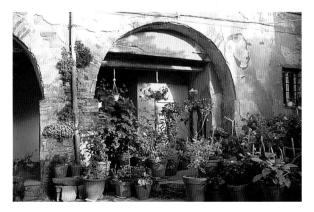

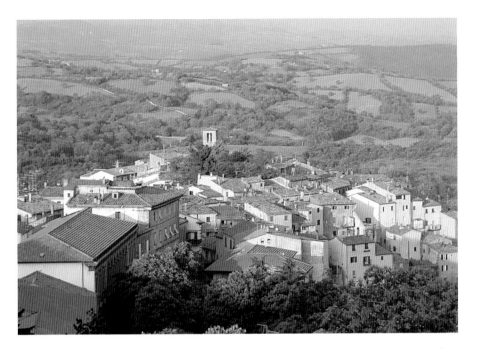

Grosseto, head to Albinia on the Aurelia, which offers a good impression of the Maremma's extensive coastal plain. The distant hills are cloaked in olive grove and Mediterranean scrub while the pine forests on the right were planted intentionally, as a backdrop to the coastal beaches.

The Albinia turn-off leads into a fertile area of fruit and vegetable plots. Once past the level-crossing fork left (to Magliano) and after a while the road starts to rise. Olive trees, dotting the pale slopes in perfect grids, dominate the scenery, while here and there chestnut trees, prized for their medicinal purposes, line the road. Remains of Etruscan settlements also appear from time to time (it is believed the Etruscans first planted the olive here) as do old vines looped between olive trees, a mixed cultivation system long since abandoned.

Magliano is reached in 15 minutes and though but 130 metres high it gives excellent views of Mount Argentario and the Isle of Giglio. Its almost intact, 15th-century city walls are quite a sight too. This is the start of Morellino country proper. As the road (to Pereta) continues to rise its curves get ever tighter and the views more panoramic. Ten minutes on you pass Mantellassi, followed shortly by Le Pupille. Past Pereta the land gets wilder, the slopes become plunges and there is more foresting. At one point is a lay-by with stunning views south to Parrina and into Lazio, east to Manciano and Pitigliano and way out to sea. Further on you pass Bargagli and a huge Roman villa, then Scansano itself. From Scansano it is a rolling descent back to Grosseto, past Pancole and Montorgiali. The round trip takes about two hours.

Above *The hill-top town of Scansano was once the summer seat of the Grosseto bureaucracy.*

Tel: 0564 592030; cl. Wed
Friendly trattoria. High regard for traditions and superb local food. Fine cheese board. Good choice of wines, also good house. Tasting menu. Seats outside. Excellent value.

Da Sandra
Magliano, Via Garibaldi, 20
Tel: 0564 592196; cl. Mon
Rich, wholesome local fare; too tasty for self-restraint.

Guido
Magliano, Via Roma, 18
Tel: 0564 592447; cl. Tue
Small, relaxing. Fine quality dishes, based on classics but with individuality. Well chosen, regional wine list. Good value.

Il Rifrullo
Scansano, Via Marconi, 3
Tel: 0564 507183; cl. Thu
Small, homely. Fine local ingredients cooked with care and inventiveness. Well chosen local wines. Seats outside. Inexpensive, good value.

PLACES OF INTEREST

Olivo della Strega, Magliano
The oldest known olive tree. Estimates of its age vary but 'several centuries' is the consensus.

Parrina to Pitigliano

PARRINA AND ENVIRONS

WINE PRODUCERS

Tenuta La Parrina
Tel: 0564 862636; fax: 0564 862626;
E, F, G
Ignore the 'Vino Etrusco' sign, this is
serious stuff. Large estate with wide
range of fruit and vegetable crops,
plus sheep and goats for cheese.
Cheery, fruity, very drinkable red;
more structured Riserva. Lively, clean
whites. Pay for tasting. Visits working

Tuscany's south west corner is often sunny when the rest is under a cloud, so can be a good bolt hole to escape a day's gloom. Mind you, a day is barely sufficient to explore the southern zones of Parrina, Ansonica Costa dell' Argentario, Capalbio and Bianco di Pitigliano; not because the viticulture is so extensive, but because it is awash with natural and historical glories it would be almost criminal to miss: the Argentario peninsula, medieval hill-top towns ... To start the trail, first take the Aurelia to Albinia and on to Quattre Strade. There turn left to enter the zone of Parrina.

PARRINA

Parrina is a small zone completely enclosed within that of Capalbio. It has just one producer, Tenuta La Parrina. The area looks flat, but the vineyards are behind, on foothill slopes and worth visiting for the views alone.

The wine comes in red, white and rosé. The red and rosé are based on Sangiovese and the white on Trebbiano with Chardonnay and/or Ansonica.

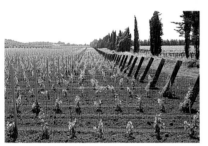

hours only. Must book. Book rooms
with estate or agency 3-4 months
prior; min. stay 4 nights in low season.
Sassotondo
Sovana
Tel: 0564 614218; fax: 0564 617714; E
Old tufa cellars but modernly
equipped. Good Bianco di Pitigliano
but highlight is red, fruit-forward
Sassotondo (Ciliegiolo/Alicante). Also
Rosso Franze (Sangiovese), San
Lorenzo (Ciliegiolo). Must book.
Book with estate; no min. stay.

ENOTECHE

Rosso e Pasioni Orbetello
Wine bar. Snacks of Bruschetta with
various toppings.
La Dispensa del Conte Pitigliano
Ghiottornia Pitigliano
Per Bacco Montemerano

EATING OUT

Orlando
Porto Santo Stefano
Tel: 0564 812788; cl. Tue in winter
Leisurely. Very good fish. Good wines.
Fabulous views from large terrace.
Not expensive.
Osteria del Lupacante
Orbetello, Corso Italia, 103
Tel: 0564 867618; cl. Tue in winter
The freshest of fish (so full menu

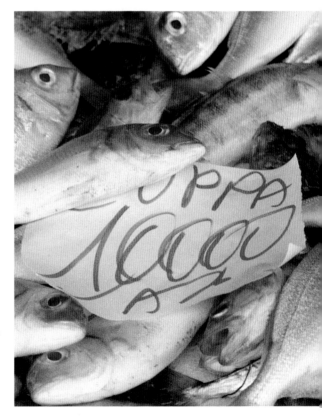

ANSONICA COSTA DELL'ARGENTARIO AND CAPALBIO

Wine from the white Ansonica grape has long been made in the area. However, Ansonica (sometimes written Ansonaca, Ansonaco, Anzonica or other variations on the theme) is a Sicilian grape, there called Inzolia, yet found nowhere else on mainland Italy. So it is reckoned that in the 18th century Sicilians who, disturbed by Spanish invasions, took flight and sailed north, taking vine material with them. Some landed on Isola del Giglio, the small island to the west where production is still concentrated, and then proceeded to the Argentario peninsula and its hinterland. Numerous Sicilian surnames in the area add weight to the theory.

Ansonica, though susceptible to disease, thrived on the stony, limestone soil but all too easily made dark coloured, hefty, stringy, oxidized wines. Although interest in the grape's potential was increasing before, the arrival of the DOC Ansonica Costa dell'Argentario in the mid-1990s was the catalyst and some good, characterful wines are now emerging.

A newer DOC, Capalbio, covering the lands between the Argentario and the Pitigliano zone, now brings the area's varietal wines made from Sangiovese, Vermentino, Cabernet Sauvignon, and Sangiovese blends into the DOC net too.

This territory is a must for its unique and eye-catching geography. Monte Argentario is a large lump of forested land,

range not always available) in relaxed atmosphere. Broad wine list. Seats outside. Not expensive.

Il Frantoio
Capalbio, Piazza Providenza, 10
Tel: 0564 896484; cl. Tue
In old oil mill. Fish- and meat-based menus, local dishes. Also bar for snacks. Good regional wine list. Seats outside.

Da Maria
Capalbio, Via Belvedere, 3
Tel: 0564 896014; cl. Tue
Long-standing, popular restaurant. High quality local dishes. Well chosen regional wines. Terrace. Mid-priced.

Il Tufo Allegro
Pitigliano, Vicolo della Costituzione, 2
Tel: 0564 616192; cl. Tue
Carved from tufa. Wine leads with huge list. Flavoursome local foods with individual touch. Inexpensive, great value.

Far left Parrina: worth visiting if only for the views. On a clear day Elba and even Corsica can be seen. Below and bottom The Isola del Giglio is the nucleus of Ansonica production. Ferries sail from Porto Santo Stefano.

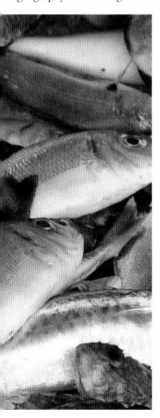

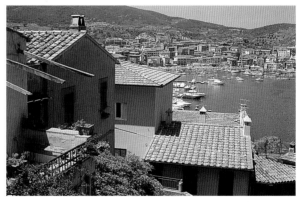

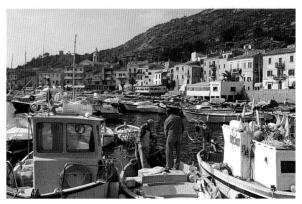

Da Caino
Montemerano, Via Chiesa, 4
*Tel: 0564 602817; cl. Thu lunch, Wed
(winter only)*
One of Italy's top-notch restaurants
and cellars. Well worth the price.

HOTELS

There are plentiful resort hotels along
the coast.
La Stellata
Saturnia, Loc. Pian del Bagno
Tel: 0564 602934; fax: 0564 602934
Owned by Terme di Saturnia but less
costly and more Tuscan, country-house
environment. Five minutes from spa.
Acquaviva
Montemerano
Tel & fax: 0564 602890
Quiet, comfortable, simple, friendly.
Well furnished rooms. Also wine estate.

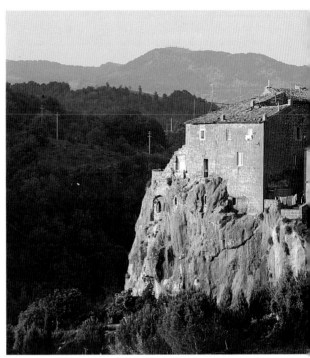

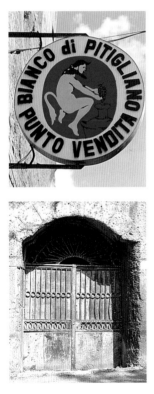

Main picture and above
*Pitigliano is built on a mass of
yellow volcanic tufa, full of holes,
many of which are used as cellars.*
Top right *Cats are often kept as
pets in Italy, but many fend for
themselves, as here, in Pitigliano.*
Right *Abundant Tuscan herbs.*

linked to the mainland by three causeways, creating two lagoons, both bird sanctuaries and one a heron reserve. The outer causeways have beaches, the middle one houses the now traffic-clogged but once Etruscan town of Orbetello.

From the Parrina road continue to the next major junction and turn left towards Albinia. Cross the Aurelia and take the northerly causeway, Tombolo della Giannella, to Porto Santo Stefano, a very well-to-do harbour town, lively even in winter and jam-packed in high summer. Continue right round the promontory, returning through the smaller, prettier Porto Ercole. The rough, twisting, partly unmade road and the splendid views make for a good two-hour trip.

Return on the middle causeway, through Orbetello, and back onto the Aurelia to head southwards past Etruscan Ansedonia, where you can still see the ancient Roman engineering solution to the port silting up. Lake Burano, another bird sanctuary follows. Then turn left to Capalbio, which glories in its 15th-century walls, still intact, circling the unspoilt medieval town and giving 360° views. Next head north to Marsiliana, a small castle perched on a prettily wooded conical hill. Turn right to Manciano, leaving the zone.

BIANCO DI PITIGLIANO
The Pitigliano wine area stretches across the southern corner of Tuscany with an additional spur overlapping half the Morellino area, looping around Scansano. You enter the zone shortly after Marsiliana, roughly at Sgrillozzo.

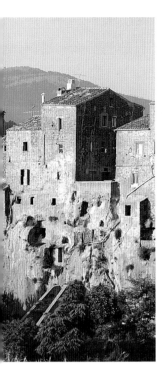

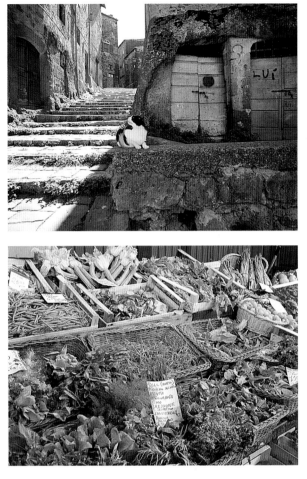

The best wine is grown on tufa soils and made mainly from Trebbiano plus one or more of a host of other varieties. The underlying neutrality of Trebbiano means the choice of complementary grape(s) can determine the style. This, therefore, varies considerably, as does quality.

The road to Pitigliano is varied, sporadically twisty, with no more than occasional vineyard patches but fascinating throughout. The town was once a thriving Jewish community, before persecution caused them to flee. Built on a mass of yellow, volcanic tufa, full of holes (many of which are used as cellars), it is quite remarkable, as is Sovana, five minutes away. Now a smallish archaeological zone of, mainly, Etruscan tombs, it was once more important than Grosseto. You could also visit Sorano, ten minutes further on, another medieval village perched on volcanic rock.

From Sovana continue roughly westward to Saturnia and from there to Montemerano. From here you can cut back to Manciano to return to Grosseto via Albinia. Otherwise turn right at the entrance to Montemerano, towards Scansano, a part of the zone where Bianco di Pitigliano overlaps Morellino di Scansano. Pass through Scansano, fork left onto a minor road to Montiano (towards Fonteblanda) and turn right again, signposted Grosseto, just before reaching the village.

La Taverna Etrusca
Sovana, Piazza del Pretorio, 16
Tel: 0564 616183; fax: 0564 614193
Central. Tiny medieval building. Small rooms. Parking. 3*.

PLACES OF INTEREST

Terme di Saturnia
Tel: 0564 601061
Italian flair at its best: luxury resort around the Saturnia spa. Daily ticket (all treatments extra) within supercomfortable (and expensive) hotel or have a hot sulphurous, mineral bath for free down the road.

SPECIAL EVENTS

Palio Marinaro
Porto Santo Stefano.
15 August. Rowing regatta with one competitor for each of the town's four quarters. Preceded by costume parade.
Wild Orchids in flower April

Monteregio di Massa Marittima

MASSA MARITTIMA

WINE PRODUCERS

Meleta
Tel: 0564 567155
Some of the area's classiest wines.
Rosso della Rocca (Sangiovese/
Cabernet) and Bianco della Rocca
(Chardonnay) lead range.

Il Pupillo
Tel: 0566 37230
18th-century cellars; varietal wines.

Massa Vecchia
Tel: 0566 915522; E
Small, highly quality-conscious estate.
Intriguing range: Monteregio Rosso

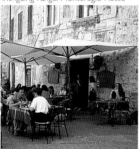

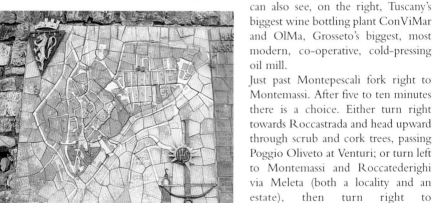

Top *Relaxing in Massa Marittima.*
Above *Just by the car park at the*
entrance to Massa Marittima, an
elegant plaque shows the layout of
this medieval town.
Right *In fine weather, the elders of*
southern Tuscan villages bring a
chair outside to sit and watch the
world go by.

Most of the wines from the area north of Grosseto are clustered under the umbrella DOC Monteregio di Massa Marittima. It covers red, white and rosé wines, including a red Riserva; red and white Vin Santo; a vino novello; and a white made almost exclusively from Vermentino. Otherwise the whites are from Trebbiano blended with all or any of Malvasia, Ansonica, Vermentino and others; the reds and rosés are mainly from Sangiovese. The area spreads from Roccastrada in the east almost to the coast, and covers much of the hilly area north of the city where soils are mainly clay, rich in skeletal remains. Vineyards are dotted here and there but it is an area of mixed agriculture with the olive dominating, as it does throughout the province.

OIL, WINE AND SCENERY

From Grosseto head northward. If you take the slower, 'old' Aurelia, running parallel to the 'new' Aurelia, it is much less busy and easier for visiting places. It is certainly worth diverting, after just a few minutes, both left to Vetulonia, once one of the most important of Etruscan cities, and still with its major necropolis; and right to Montepescali, a captivating medieval hill-top village. From the road you can also see, on the right, Tuscany's biggest wine bottling plant ConViMar and OlMa, Grosseto's biggest, most modern, co-operative, cold-pressing oil mill.

Just past Montepescali fork right to Montemassi. After five to ten minutes there is a choice. Either turn right towards Roccastrada and head upward through scrub and cork trees, passing Poggio Oliveto at Venturi; or turn left to Montemassi and Roccatederighi via Meleta (both a locality and an estate), then turn right to Roccastrada. At 475 metres this is a fabulous vantage point; sometimes, on clear days, the vineyards of Montalcino to the east are visible. Head straight back down (signposted Grosseto) and, just by Montepescali, take the right turn towards Follonica onto the old Aurelia (signposted Castiglione della Pescaia).

You could divert to Grilli to see the San Luigi *frantoio.* Otherwise pass the hill-top village of Gavorrano (left), turn left at the second signpost for Bagno di Gavorrano and go straight towards Scarlino. (The turn-off for central Scarlino leads to a sequence of tight bends up to the village, perched

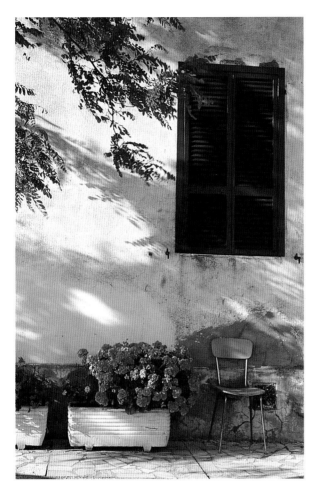

Riserva; Terziere (Alicante); Le Veglie di Neri, (Aleatico passito); Patrizia Bartolino (Sauvignon passito); Ariento (Vermentino). Must book.

Moris Farms see p102

Harald Bremer
Tel: 0564 939060
In Vetulonia. Bremer is a prickly character and a perfectionist – and the wines reap the benefits. Monteregio Rosso, Vetluna (Cabernet).

OLIVE OIL PRODUCERS

Poggio Oliveto
Valeria Cittadini is fanatical about oil. No effort is spared, no detail ignored to ensure it is in perfect condition. The *frantoio* is strictly traditional, no technique that could compromise quality is countenanced. The oil is splendid.

Frantoio San Luigi
Modern cold-pressing plant but traditional granite wheels. Well set up for visitors. Food can be provided.

EATING OUT

Bracali
Massa Marittima, Loc. Ghirlanda
Tel: 0566 902318; cl. Tue
Elegant, tranquil restaurant of supreme quality. Original dishes, light and flavoursome. Great wine list. Seats outside. Not overly expensive and good value.

Da Tronca
Massa Marittima, Via Porte, 5
Tel: 0566 901991; eves only, cl. Wed
Friendly trattoria. Local dishes. Broad wine list. Inexpensive. Good value.

Hotel Corallo
Castiglione delle Pescaia, Via Sauro, 1
Tel: 0564 933668; cl. Tue in winter
Classic Maremma fish dishes with individual touches. Good wines.

HOTELS

Corallo
Castiglione della Pescaia
Tel: 0564 933668; fax: 0564 936268
Small, quiet, characterful. Good restaurant (see above). 3*.

Il Sole
Massa Marittima, Corso Libertà, 43
Tel: 0566 901971; fax: 0565 901959
Renovated medieval building. 3*.

COASTAL RESORTS

Castiglione della Pescaia
Fishing port; long, fine, sandy beach; medieval village above.

Punta Ala Superb beach and resort facilities.

Cala Violino Quiet bay.

Follonica Major resort. Excellent white sand beach.

on a pine-carpeted hill and with great sea views.) Just ahead on the left is Il Pupillo. Turn right, back across the Aurelia to Cura Nova, where, just on the right, is the large estate Moris Farms. Then continue to Massa Marittima.

MASSA MARITTIMA

This terrific 10th-century village, 380 metres high and built to a careful plan, was once called Massa Metallorum and was the prosperous centre of a silver, copper and other metal mining area. It is now named 'Marittima' to distinguish it from the Massa near Carrara (see p125) and is dominated by its large, central piazza around which all the municipal and church buildings cluster, leaving space to admire the surroundings, wander, grab a bite to eat, or simply sit and people-watch. By the side of the cathedral is a wonderful old cellar belonging to Moris Farms, carved from the friable rock of the massif. It is open daily (except Wednesdays) and at the entrance there is a range of food products and ceramics, plus wines, of course, to buy.

Val di Cornia

VAL DI CORNIA

WINE PRODUCERS

Jacopo Banti
Campiglia Marittima
Tel: 0565 838802; E
Top-sited vineyards at 250-300m,
overlooking coast, with fine views.
Emphasis on quality and style. Two
white Val di Cornias, two red, plus
Ceragiolo (Ciliegiolo). Also lemon-
flavoured olive oil.

Gualdo del Re
Suvereto, Loc. Notri
Tel: 0565 829888; Italian only
Smallish estate. Tightly pruned,
densely planted vineyard; well
equipped cellars. Rich, rounded, ripe
wines. Val di Cornia red and white,
Gualdo del Re (Sangiovese), Federico
Primo (Cabernet/Merlot), Valentina
(Vermentino), Lumen (Pinot Bianco).

Tua Rita
Suvereto, Loc. Notri
Tel: 0565 49471
High quality estate with intense, deep,
complex wines. Giusto di Notri (Cabernet/
Merlot), Redigaffi (Merlot), Perlato del
Bosco red (from Sangiovese, old vines)
and white Sileno (Riesling/Chardonnay/
Traminer) and others.

The centre of the Val di Cornia, around which most of its estates are clustered, is Suvereto. Many vines grow on the lowest, gentlest slopes within a stone's throw of the distinctly unpicturesque broad Cornia Valley, which is crossed by several tributaries as well as the river Cornia itself. However, sea breezes blowing along the valley ventilate the vineyards and temper the climate; most vines are low-trained and tightly pruned, and many enjoy higher slopes further from the river, so prospects for good wines are better than at first sight.

The reds, like most in Tuscany, are predominantly from Sangiovese and there is also a Riserva. Optionally, one or more of Canaiolo, Ciliegiolo, Cabernet Sauvignon or Merlot can be added. The whites, as usual, are based on Trebbiano Toscano. Less usually, 15–30 percent of Vermentino is added. Other varieties that may be included are Pinot Bianco, Pinot Grigio, Clairette and the local Biancone (found also on Elba and Corsica) as well as the more common Malvasia and Ansonica. Some producers also make a rosé (from Sangiovese).

You could rush up to the area on the Aurelia then cut inland. However if your last port of call was Massa Marittima (see p109) there is a wonderful cut-through across remarkably diverse terrain. Head down from Massa Marittima following signs for Siena. At the bottom of the

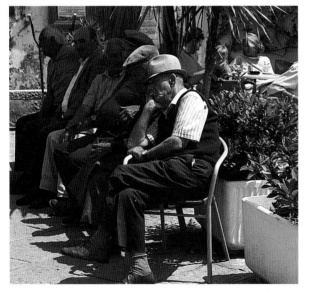

Above *Not just a relaxing shady spot, but a chance to discuss the important matters in life.*
Right *The Val di Cornia valley.*

Above right *The Val di Cornia combines vine, olive and wheat.*
Below right *Summer in Elba, all types of tomatoes for sale.*

descent, there appears to be a simple choice between two almost parallel roads both shooting forwards. But there is a garage on the left, and just beside it a tiny, single-track road which requires almost a U-turn to get onto it. As you do, a small, almost illegible yellow sign confirms that this is the way to Suvereto. Apart from intensively cultivated small plots of mixed crops and wooded slopes there are numerous large, healthy cork trees. The road leads through Montebamboli and a series of curves. Once it straightens out, go straight over the crossroads to San Lorenzo, where you'll see the greatest concentration of vineyards, low, neat and tidy, since Montalcino. A road of sorts cuts across from here to Suvereto, but it is devilish to find, and is little more than a rutted track going straight through a couple of the

Bulichella
Suvereto, Loc. Bulichella
Tel: 0565 829892
Organic. Also organic oil, fruit, vegetables, cereals, honey, jams. On sale in Il Bucchero, Via Magenta, Suvereto.

Ambrosini
Suvereto, Loc. Tabarò
Tel: 0565 829301; Italian only
Range includes, curiously, red from eastern Italy's Abruzzo region's Montepulciano grape (no connection with the town).

Montepeloso
Suvereto, Loc. Montepeloso
Tel: 0565 828180
Suvereto's rising star. Val di Cornia red and white plus Nardo (Sangiovese/Cabernet).

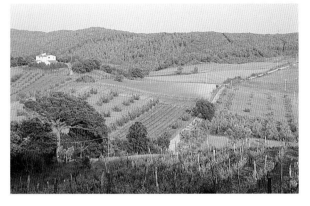

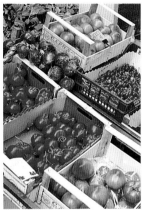

ELBA

WINE PRODUCERS

Acquabona
Portoferraio, Loc. Acquabona
Tel: 0565 933013
Elba's leading estate. Wide range of varieties, including Ansonica. Leading grape Aleatico, powerful and complex.

La Chiusa
Portoferraio, Loc. Magazzini
Tel: 0565 933046; E, F
Elba red, white, rosé and three *passiti* from Ansonica, Aleatico and Trebbiano/ Moscato. Phone first. Groups must book. Book rooms with estate 3-4 months prior. (In Germany bookings must be through Agenzia Cultura.)

ENOTECHE

Furio Venturina
Dei Difficili Suvereto

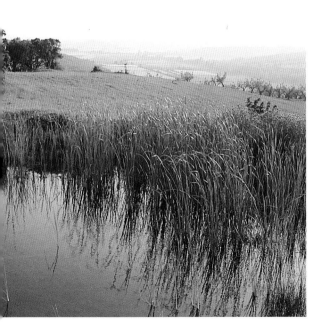

Right *Portoferraio, Elba.*
Below A *calm moment in the fish
market in Castiglione della Pescaia.*
Far right *Not often do palm trees
punctuate a vineyard, as in Elba.*
Below right *Despite Piombino's
ugliness, there are beautiful corners.*

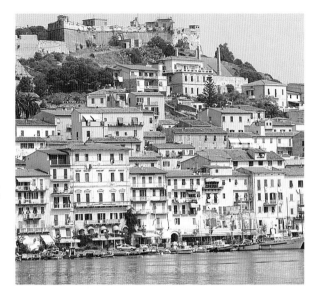

EATING OUT

Eno-Oliteca Ombrone
Suvereto, Piazza dei Giudici, 1
Tel: 0565 829336; cl. Mon
Old oil mill. Classic Tuscan dishes pre-
pared with aplomb. Large range of oils.
Oil list as well as (good) wine list. Seats
outside. Mid-priced.
Il Canovaccio
Campiglia Marittima, Via Vecchio Asilo, 1
*Tel: 0565 838449; eves only, cl. Tue in
winter*
Long-standing trattoria. Lots of
starters and primi; no main courses.

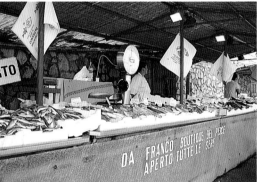

Mainly vegetables and fish. Pizza avail-
able. Good desserts. Shortish, well-
chosen, regional wine list.
Il Garibaldo Innamorato
Piombino, Via Garibaldi, 5
Tel: 0565 49410; cl. Mon
Simply designed, friendly place.
Fish-based menu; varies with availab-
ility in local market. Taster portions
available. Well-selected wines.
Not costly.
Lucumone
Populonia, Al Castello
Tel: 0565 29471; cl. Tue lunch, Mon
Smart restaurant, splendidly sited,
seasonally changing menu, mainly fish.
Mid-priced, good value.
Emanuel
Portoferraio, Loc. Enfola
Tel: 0565 939003; cl. Wed in winter
Classic Elba fish dishes. Daily menu.
Tasting menu. Wide-ranging wine
list but plenty of Elba wines too.
Good value.

Cornia's tributaries. Even though
these could be dried up in summer
it is probably better to return to the
crossroads, and fork left towards
Suvereto. You pass through
another intensely cultivated patch
of vineyard before the road begins
to climb into the town itself.

Suvereto's streets curve round the
hillside forming a set of concentric
half-circles crossed by steep cut-
throughs. Romanesque and
medieval buildings combine with
marble-fronted buildings, making it unusually attractive.
Don't be fooled by the signs to 'Belvedere', though. They
lead to a hamlet ten minutes above Suvereto – not a lay-by
with a great panorama. From Suvereto you could cut
straight through to the Bolgheri area (see p114) on a tiny
twisting road towards Sassetta, or zoom down past
Campiglia Marittima and Venturina towards the coastal
town of Piombino.

PIOMBINO

Piombino is an eyesore. It is a heavily industrial area with
metal smelters pumping out fumes and polluting the atmosphere, although it does have a reasonably well preserved
centre. Unfortunately, if you want to take a ferry across
to the isle of Elba, you have no choice but to fight through
Piombino's traffic and its fumes (unless you sail
from Livorno, much further north). You also need to
get within sniffing distance of it to visit the Etruscan mira-
cle of Populonia.

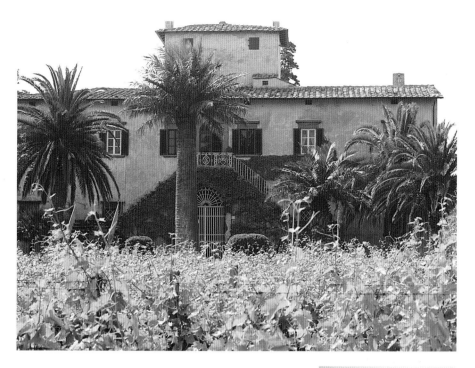

If signs to this ancient site prove elusive, follow those for San Vincenzo until a left turn to Populonia appears. Within a couple of minutes you pass a major necropolis, with tombs from all periods and of all types. The custodian (who speaks only Italian) will open the area for you on request. The road skates the coast, rising through woods. Watch the roadside carefully as you go and you will see an ancient head carved into the rock.

Populonia in Etruscan times was, like today, a centre of ore extraction, though clearly less brutish. Its most significant structure now is the peaceful, squat, round-turreted Medici castle, and its coastline remains a confirmed beauty-spot.

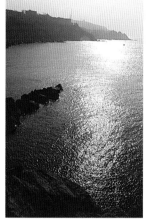

ELBA

Elba is best visited out of season. The thousands of cars going across to the island in summer can turn its panoramic narrow twisting roads into gridlocked frustration.

The island is rich in mineral reserves. Many are ferrous compounds or semi-precious stones, so for something more active than sunbathing (most beaches are rocky, a few pebbly or sandy) try a treasure hunt.

The wines, reputedly, also have a minerally tang. It is not too pronounced, though, as most are made light and easy, to satisfy the thirsts of the many holiday-makers, who drink practically all the production. The reds, as ever, are mainly Sangiovese, the whites based on Trebbiano, although there is also some white Ansonica (and a sweet *passito* version), a little Vin Santo, some sparkling wine and a sweet red made from the Aleatico variety.

HOTELS

Many Elba hotels are closed in winter and booked solid in summer. Plan ahead if overnighting there.

FOOD SHOPPING

Covered Market
Portoferraio, Via delle Galeazze.
Well worth a browse. Fish especially eye-catching.

Gastronomia I Parrigiana
Portoferraio
Wide choice of tempting delicacies.

Bolgheri

THE WINES

Just the thought of the Bolgheri area can be enough to bring a frisson of excitement to Italian wine enthusiasts. The idea of seeing the home of Sassicaia, the estate that, reputedly almost single-handedly convinced a doubting world that Italy could produce top-class wines, draws folk from all around. But don't get too keyed up. Sassicaia and its rival, the almost equally famous Ornellaia, are two of the few estates in Italy which do not encourage visitors – it is not even worth trying.

Strangely, the Bolgheri area does not look or feel much like a wine zone. Most is practically flat and very close to the sea, although hills do rise up behind. The soil is mainly thick clay, naturally more suited to olive or fruit trees. Vines have been planted in stonier areas where there is better drainage.

The DOC of Bolgheri was created so that renegades like Sassicaia could fit into the system. Its controls are stricter than most on yields, but liberal on grape varieties. Bolgheri Rosso can contain up to 70 percent Sangiovese, 70 percent Merlot or 80 percent Cabernet Sauvignon, allowing a wide variation of styles – a trend that other areas are starting to follow. Bolgheri Bianco, from Trebbiano, Vermentino or Sauvignon, has similar freedom in varietal make-up. There

Right *Sassicaia's cellars are at the end of the 5km-long Strada di Cipressi. This cypress-lined avenue, planted in 1801, was immortalized by Carducci in a poem familiar to every Italian school child.*

Below *The grapes of Bolgheri are subject to tight controls over the weight of crop per hectare, number of vines per hectare, weight of crop per vine and volume of juice.*

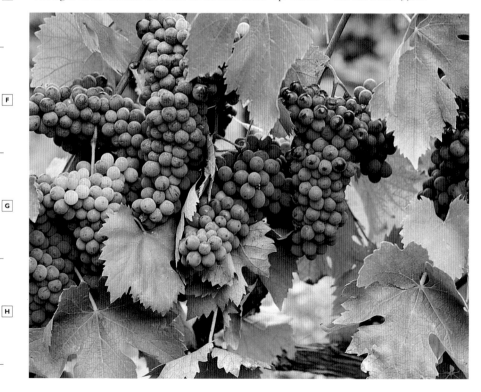

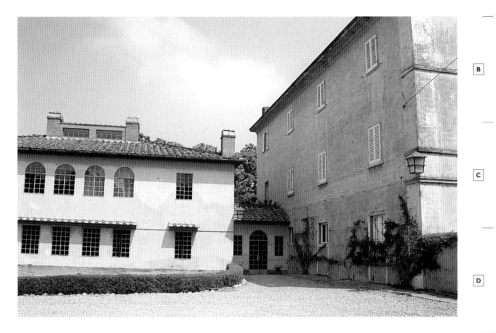

Bolgheri

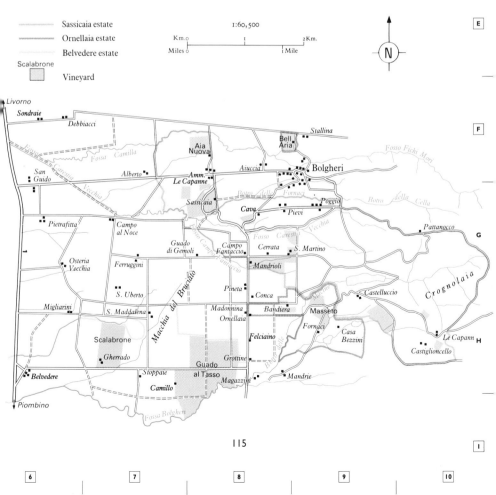

Right *The medieval village of*
Bolgheri.
Far right *A vineyard worker*
carefully tends the strictly controlled
vineyards of Bolgheri.

BOLGHERI

WINE PRODUCERS

Sassicaia
(Officially 'Tenuta San Guido')
Mostly Cabernet Sauvignon, the vines
were bought from Château Lafite in
the 1940s and the wines are massive
and extremely long-lived. Priced
accordingly.

Tenuta dell'Ornellaia
Cabernet Sauvignon with Merlot and
Cabernet Franc. Masseto (Merlot) and
whites receive rapturous praise.

Grattamacco
Tel: 0565 763840; fax: 0565 763217;
E, F
Approachable, drinkable, affordable
wines of high quality and individuality.
Must book. Book rooms with estate
two months prior.

Le Macchiole
Tel: 0565 766092; Italian only
Top-quality site, fine-quality reds:
concentrated, powerful and long.
Whites good too Must book.

Michele Satta
Tel: 0565 763894
Classy wines of personality. Satta
sustainer of Sangiovese.

Tenuta Belvedere
Tel: 0565 749735
Another branch of the Antinori
empire. Guado al Tasso (Cabernet) is
the flagship; Vermentino and rosé
Scalabrone both characterful

ENOTECHE

Tognoni Bolgheri
Del Borgo Castagneto Carducci
Maestrini Donoratico
Bolgheri and Castagneto Carducci
have wine shops with good ranges of
Bolgheri wines.

EATING OUT

Da Ugo
Castagneto Carducci, Via Pari, 3/a
Tel: 0565 763746; cl. Mon
Long-standing, well renowned
restaurant. Simple, flavoursome,
local foods; fish- or meat-based
menus. Large and well-balanced
wine list.

Bagnoli
Castagneto Carducci, Loc. Bagnoli
Tel: 0565 763630; cl. Wed
Warm, family-run trattoria.

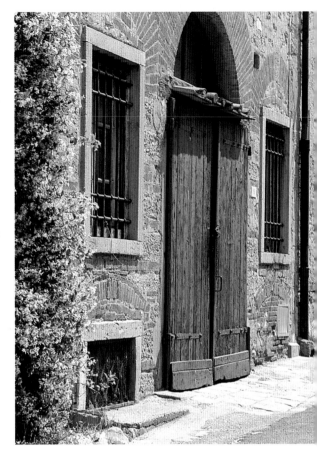

are also varietal versions from Vermentino and Sauvignon,
red Vin Santo (called Occhio di Pernice) and a rosé.
Sassicaia itself forms a Bolgheri sub-zone and requires at
least 80 percent Cabernet Sauvignon.

THE VINEYARDS

From Populonia, head north along the coast to San Vincenzo,
a sizeable resort with a long but fairly narrow beach. From
there take the Aurelia (old or new) to Donoratico. In summer
this stretch is packed, so leave plenty of time for what in winter is a 20-minute hop. Follow signs initially for Castagneto
Carducci, then for Bolgheri. As soon as you leave the Aurelia
you are in the Bolgheri zone and very shortly pass the estate
of Michele Satta. After a sharp left turn the vineyards of the
highly regarded Grattamacco are visible up to the right. A little further on to the left, 100–200 metres from the road, is the
Guado del Tasso vineyard of Piero Antinori's Tenuta
Belvedere. Drive slowly and keep a watch to the right: after a
few minutes the smart entrance to Ornellaia appears, a long,
imposing drive behind firmly locked gates. Opposite is Le
Macchiole, signposted Contessine. A little past Ornellaia, on

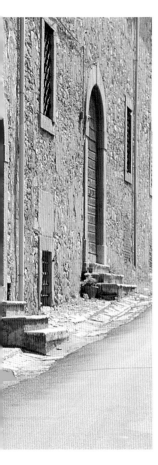

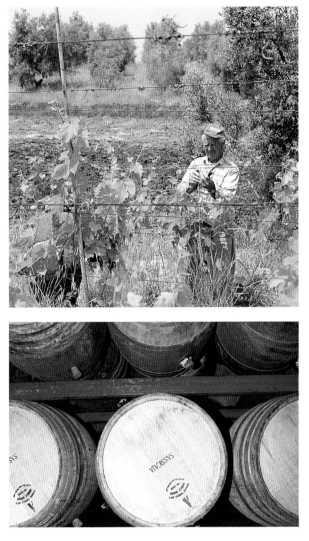

Right *In some ways Bolgheri resembles Bordeaux – indeed Marchese Niccolò della Rochetta of Sassicaia created the wine partly out of his admiration for the fine Bordeaux châteaux.*

the right, is a tidy vineyard with very low, tightly pruned vines. This belongs to Sassicaia – it is not marked in any way, though many less illustrious estates along the route are. The previously straight road then begins to wind: where it straightens out again there is another Sassicaia vineyard, this time on the left.

The road then crosses another which runs from the sea to Bolgheri village. Its entirety, five kilometres, is lined with cypress trees. Divert left onto this avenue to see Sassicaia's cellars, an unmarked, large pink shed on the left, just before meeting the Aurelia again. Turn back, branching left to Bibbona just before reaching the medieval Bolgheri village. More Sassicaia vines are about 300 metres along on the left. Continue to Bibbona, also medieval and worth exploring, and on to Casale Marittima, bringing you to the Montescudaio zone.

Comforting, substantial local dishes; good range of Bolgheri wines. Not costly.

Gambero Rosso
San Vincenzo, Piazza della Vittoria, 13
Tel: 0565 701021; cl. Mon eve, Tue
Some rate this the best restaurant in Italy; it's certainly in the top ten. Food, wine, service, ambience, all is simply fabulous. Though, rightly, costly the value is marvellous.

FOOD SHOPPING

Verde Negozio Donoratico
Fruit, vegetables, bread, prepared foodstuffs; all organic.

MONTESCUDAIO AND VOLTERRA

WINE PRODUCERS

Poggio Gagliardo
Montescudaio, Loc. Poggio Gagliardo
Tel: 0586 630661; E, F, G
Large estate. Well made, characterful wines. Three versions of white Montescudaio, three of the red. Accepts on-spec visits. Book rooms with estate.

Fattoria Sorbaiano
Montecatini Val di Cecina
Tel: 0586 30243
High quality. Montescudaio red and white: fruity and drinkable. Selections Lucestraia (white) and Rosso delle Miniere (red): denser and more complex.

Montescudaio and Volterra

MONTESCUDAIO

The red wines of Montescudaio are, as usual, based on Sangiovese but follow old precepts and contain 15-25 percent of white grapes, giving a fresh, light touch. The whites are Trebbiano with, mostly, Malvasia and Vermentino. There is also a Vin Santo. The vineyards cluster along the Cecina river and around the villages of Casale Marittima, Guardistallo and Montescudaio. The best way to get a feel of the area is to travel through these in turn, then head west, down through the hills to Cecina (and its devilish one-way system). Then turn back eastward, along the river to Volterra.

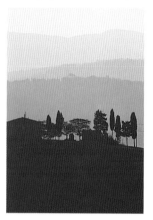

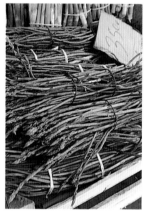

The route is punctuated by occasional eye-catching views, graceful and tranquil. There are also odd outcrops of bare, blue-grey clay: the first signs of the characteristic 'moonscape' that surrounds Volterra.

Left Fresh asparagus piled high on a local market stall.
Right, far left and below It is almost impossible not to be captivated by Volterra. From its ancient walls there are 360° views of the surrounding countryside.

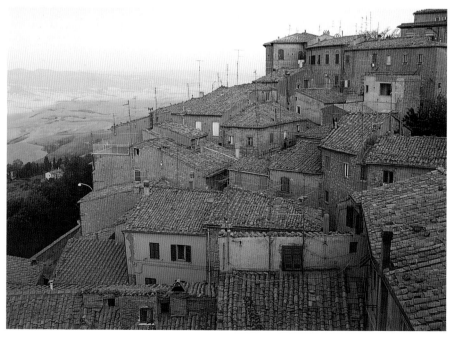

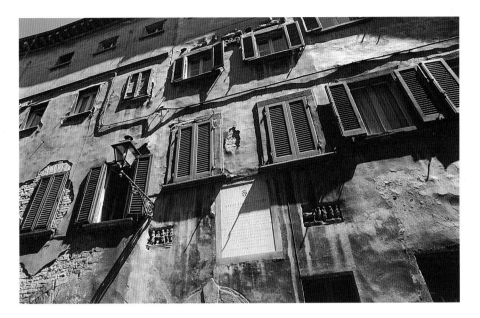

A brief detour up towards Guardistallo gives enthralling glimpses of Volterra and, on the return, a marvellous panorama over the whole Cecina valley. Back along the river, vineyards become increasingly sparse and cling solely to the right bank where there are sunnier, south-facing slopes; sun-flowers carpet the valley floor. As the road begins to rise towards Volterra and (depending on season) the 'moonscape' becomes ever eerier, you pass Saline di Volterra, site of the old salt mines that kept the Medicis wealthy.

VOLTERRA

Volterra, perched at almost 550 metres, rests on 3,000 years of history. It was the capital of Etruria, then a major Roman town (the amphitheatre and baths still survive). Huge stretches of the old city walls are still intact (and you can walk right round them, with 360° views) as is a massive Etruscan gate, Porta all'Arco. The well-preserved, narrow streets, pedestrianized, are mainly medieval, though with Etruscan and Roman relics, and are a walker's delight. Alabaster min-ing and sculpting is important – as it has been since Etruscan times, and the Guarnacci (one of three major museums) has a fine collection of ancient alabaster urns. Volterra is also a good base for a trip to San Gimignano (see p74).

From Volterra, make for Montecatini Val di Cecina. As you sweep through the beautiful steep hills you may spot what look like plumes of smoke in the distance. These are sites of geo-thermic electricity generators, a clever process that harnesses the power of underground volcanic hot springs. After the road merges with another, it skates the wine zone, now on your left side only. Continue, towards Pontedera, out of Montescudaio and into the Era valley.

EATING OUT

Il Frantoio
Montescudaio, Via della Madonna, 11
Tel: 0586 650381; eves only cl. Mon
Friendly, family-run trattoria. Fish- and meat-based menus, good quality and good value. Good choice of local wines.

Scacciapensieri
Cecina, Via Verdi, 22
Tel: 0586 680900; cl. Mon
Ornate restaurant. Excellent fish. Large wine list and good service. Rather costly.

Trattoria del Sacco Fiorentino
Volterra, Piazza XX Settembre, 18
Tel: 0588 88537; cl. Fri
Friendly. Intriguing dishes based in tra-dition but inventive. Large, wide-rang-ing wine list. Inexpensive, good value.

HOTEL

Villa Nenci
Volterra, Borgo Santo Stefano
Tel: 0588 86386; fax: 0588 806601
Just outside town. 17th-century villa. Large, comfortable rooms. Wine tast-ings. Garden, pool. Parking. Good 3*.

FOOD SHOPPING

La Scalinata Montescudaio
Bread, baked in old wooden oven.
Frantoio I Massi Guardistallo, Loc. I Massi. Cold-pressed, organic olive oil.
Lischetto Volterra (towards Montecatini)
Farm shop for good cheeses, oil, honey.

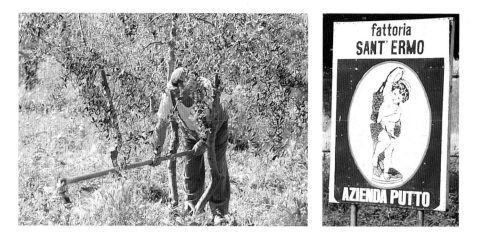

SPECIAL EVENTS

Polenta Festival Guardistallo
Second Sunday of October
Wine Festival Montescudaio
First Sunday of October

PISA AND ENVIRONS

WINE PRODUCERS

Moos
Soiana
Tel & fax: 0587 654180; E, F, G
Tiny estate, endless amounts of tlc
expended in vineyards. Dense, tight,
long-lived, impressive wines: Soianello
(80% Sangiovese), Fontestina (95%
Sangiovese), Soiano Bianco (Vermentino).
Must book. Book rooms with estate.

Tenuta di Ghizzano
Tel: 0587 630096; E, F
Good wines, continuously improving.
Best known for Veneroso
(Sangiovese/Cabernet). Pay for tast-
ings. Must book. Book rooms with
estate 2 months prior

Badia di Morrona
Tel: 0587 658505; fax: 0587 655127; G
Large, well-sited estate. Steadily
improving wines led by Vignalta
(Sangiovese), N'Antia (Cabernet/
Merlot/Sangiovese). Book rooms with
agency, Tuscan Holiday.

Fattoria Uccelliera
*Tel: 050 662747; fax: 0587 662663;
E, F, G*
Good quality, fruit-driven, attractive,
well-made, mid-weight wines. Large
range. May pay for tastings. Visits
restricted hours. Book rooms with
estate two months prior.

Tenuta del Terriccio
Castellina Marittima, Loc. Badie
Tel: 050 699709; E, F
Huge estate. Horse rearing. Rich, big,

Pisa and environs

COLLINE PISANE

The Pisan Hills, or the hills of Pisa's province, form a Chianti sub-zone. The idea of a Chianti, eternally associated with eastern Tuscany, Florence and Siena, coming from the maritime republic of Pisa is too much of a contradiction for the average Italian, and Chianti Colline Pisane has been regarded as something of a joke. In addition, most develop-ments in the area have been instigated by non-Tuscans who have moved in, although now the Pisans are getting their act together too. Even so, the top estates have almost entirely turned their backs on the handicap of the Chianti denomi-nation, preferring to use a prominent individual name together with the more neutral, broad-based Colli dell'Etruria Centrale. The area stretches from the coast inland to San Miniato and from the Montescudaio zone north to the Arno Valley.

Its heartland, with soils of mineral-rich, hard clay, is sur-prisingly unknown and relatively few travellers cross it — a boon for those who do, especially because the scenery belies the ugliness of the approaches. A white wine, Bianco Pisano di San Torpé, is also produced in the area.

THE VINEYARDS

Heading northward from Volterra you enter the Colline Pisane by a cypress-topped knoll to the right, about ten minutes from the Pontèdera fork. Single rows of vines then start to appear: these traditionally demarcated fields or prop-erties. To explore the eastern half of the area keep straight on, past the Terricola junction, then cross the river to the beautiful old town of Peccioli, from there, just a short if tor-tuous hop to Ghizzano. Otherwise, turn left to Terriciola and its more uplifting backdrop, which marks the start of the Colline Pisane's heartland. The first vineyard, part of the

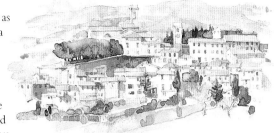

Belvedere estate, soon appears then, as the road curves leftwards, there is a sudden explosion of vineyard.

Continue, through the village and along the hill crest to Morrona, passing the cellar of Badia di Morrona. Just beyond is a vantage point with views of the church and the best vineyards. Within minutes you come into Soiana, another tiny village and home of the Pisan Hills' best wines. From there, head down towards Ponsacco, branching off left to Lari. At this point it becomes clear how protected Soiana and the other central villages are from dominant, sea-borne weather systems. You cross three hill ridges in quick succession, each dominated by once feudal estates, before feeling any cooler, moister coastal air. The twists of the first rise, the steep road to Lari, give some splendid views of terraced vineyard, with Soiana up in front and Lari, with its castle, to the right. From Lari the road plunges, then rises to Crespina. From there is another swift descent and ascent to Fauglia, passing the Uccelliera estate, whose cellars are along the valley floor. On the approach to

modern-styled wines. Reds based on Cabernet; whites on Chardonnay and Sauvignon. Pay for tastings. Must book.

San Gervasio
Palaia, Loc. San Gervasio
Tel: 0587 483360; E, F, G
Up-and-coming, mid-sized, quality-conscious estate. Sirio (Sangiovese/Cabernet), Mama (Vermentino/Chardonnay) and others. Book rooms with estate 3-4 months prior.

Far left, left and below Even when coastal Tuscany is throbbing, the Pisan hills retain their tranquility.

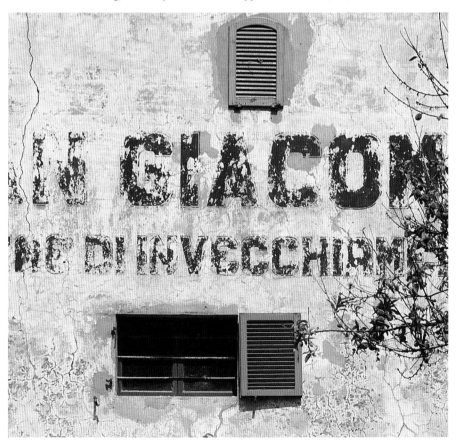

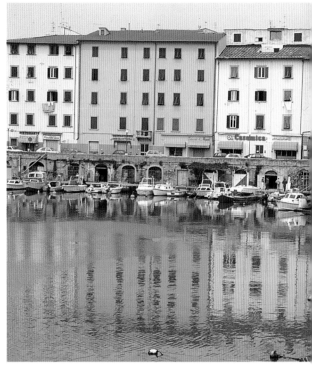

EATING OUT

La Gattaiola
Fauglia, Vicolo San Lorenzo, 2-4
Tel: 050 650852; cl. Mon
Seasonally varying menu; fresh, local
ingredients. Wide wine range. Tasting
room. Not costly.

Ciglieri
Livorno, Via O. Franchini, 38
Tel: 0586 508194; cl. Wed
Livorno's top place. Inventive, intrigu-
ing fish dishes; enthusiasm and friend-
liness throughout. Tasting menus (3).
Fine wine list. Not overly expensive.

Enoteca DOC
Livorno, Via Goldoni, 40-44
Tel: 0586 887583; cl. Mon
Huge wine range. Plentiful good
snacks. Also full meals in the evening.

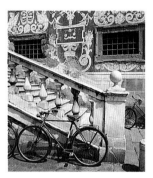

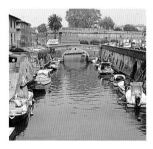

L'Antica Venezia
Livorno, Via dei Bagnetti, 1
Tel: 0586 887353; cl. Sun, Mon
In old centre. Flavoursome and very
fresh fish dishes. Short but reliable
wine list. Remarkable value.

L'Artilafo
Pisa, Via Volturno, 38
Tel: 050 27010; eves only, cl. Wed
Richly flavoured, beautifully presented
fish dishes. Excellent desserts. Wines
displayed round room. Seats outside.

La Mescita
Pisa, Via Cavalca, 2
Tel: 050 544294; cl. Mon
Small, friendly trattoria in old centre.
Excellent wine list: local, regional,

Fauglia you also pass Scopicci. Next, descend once more to
Accaiolo, then across to Torretta. You could then go straight
to Livorno. Otherwise, delay the agony by diverting southward to Rosignano Marittima then cutting across to take the
thrilling coast road back north.

LIVORNO

Unlike the sybaritic sandy beaches of further south, the upper
Livorno coast is stark and rocky. The little promontory of
Castiglioncello in particular is good for a stroll, wind-blown or
sun-drenched. In contrast. Livorno town is a huge port and
the usual harbour-side decay has permeated much of the city,
making the attractive parts small oases between urban sprawl
and marine seediness: in short, distinctly avoidable. The com-
pensation is for shoppers, with better choice and prices than in
Pisa. The pivotal sights are the Fortezza Vecchia and the
Fortezza Nuova. The latter, built in 1590, is now dedicated to
leisure, unlike the canals surrounding it.

PISA

Pisa is just 15 minutes' drive north of Livorno. Forget the dreary
approaches, the erratic signposting, the atmosphere self-satis-
fied and smug, but the focal point, the Piazza del Duomo, also
called the *Piazza dei Miracoli*, which attracts millions of
tourists and billions of lire a year, is miraculous indeed.
However many photographs you have seen, however many

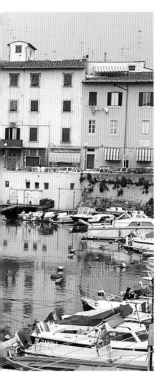

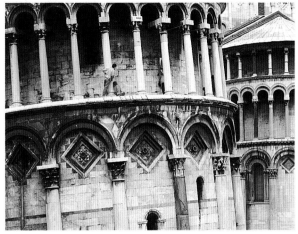

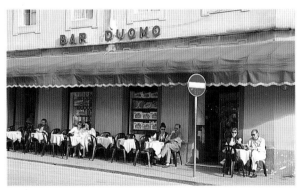

Above *Weights have been loaded onto the ground to one side of the tower in an attempt to straighten it.* Left and far left (bottom) *The port of Livorno is important commercially, but the Livornese escape the grind by going to nearby resorts Ardenza and Argignano.* Far left (top) *Palazzo dei Cavalieri, Pisa.*

national. Wine by the glass plus cheese/salami snacks available late evening. Inexpensive, great value.

Osteria dei Cavalieri
Pisa, Via San Frediano, 16
Tel: 050 580858; cl. Sat lunch, Sun
For quick but good, sustaining single course at lunchtime or the full works in the evening: local and regional classics cooked with aplomb. Wide-ranging wine list. Fairly priced.

HOTELS

Livorno is probably not the cheeriest place to overnight and Pisa's hotels rarely rise above the norm, so try:

Villa delle Rose
Pescia, Via del Castellare, 21
Tel: 0572 451301; fax: 0572 444033
Peaceful, in 18th-century villa. Large, well-furnished rooms and bathrooms. Gardens. Parking. 3*

FOOD SHOPPING

Pasticceria Fornai Pontedera
Vast range including local sweetmeats, notably Schiacciata di Pasqua.
Covered market Livorno, Scali Sassi
Plentiful fish, meat, cereals.
Da Cecco Livorno, Via Cavalletti
Torteria Gagarin Livorno, Via del Cardinale
Both for great *cecina* and *farinata* (chickpea and corn flour based snack foods respectively).
Piazza Vettovaglie Market
Pisa
Plentiful fruit and veg.
Gastronomia Simi
Pisa, Via San Martino
Gastronomia Gratin
Pisa, Via Crispi
Both for good prepared foods of all types.

times you have visited, however many tourists are cluttering the pathways, the Leaning Tower and its adjacent cathedral and baptistery stop you in your tracks. You even forget the ranks of tacky stalls all around, all selling identical tourist gear.

It is probably just as well that visitors are no longer allowed up the tower. Emerging from its narrow, sloping, slippery spiral staircase, onto a slanting arcaded ledge, with nothing between you and the ground is unsettling to say the least.

The Arno sweeps gracefully through the city, the smart buildings on either side providing a sheltered atmosphere. The piazzas are terrific, the churches majestic; shopping is good but expensive and the centre is compact, lively and relaxed. Pisa is not bad at all.

North of Pisa

From Pisa head north towards the coast, the Tuscan riviera. Resort towns (Viareggio and smart Forte dei Marmi are the best known) almost run into each other. The wide sandy beach is neatly carved into separate areas owned by hotels or franchises, each with its own style and colour of neatly serried changing cabins, umbrellas and loungers. Hotel beaches are for guests only; for the others you pay by the day or half-day for access and extra for facilities. There are odd stretches of 'public' beach, unadorned but free, but you'll need to search hard (try Lido di Camaiore). Out of season it all looks quite jolly. In season it is a seething mass of hedonistic sun-worshippers, cars and motorbikes.

As soon as you tire of resort-land, cut over to the Aurelia on any of the larger side-roads to head for the two tiny wine areas that form the main purpose of this trip, although Carrara risks stealing their thunder. The large, smooth, many-hued marble blocks that line the road or sit on the backs of lorries inevitably draw your eyes and you risk missing the vineyards completely. The first, Candia dei Colli Apuani, begins just north of Forte dei Marmi, straddling the hills on the right, the Alpi Apuane. The wines are white,

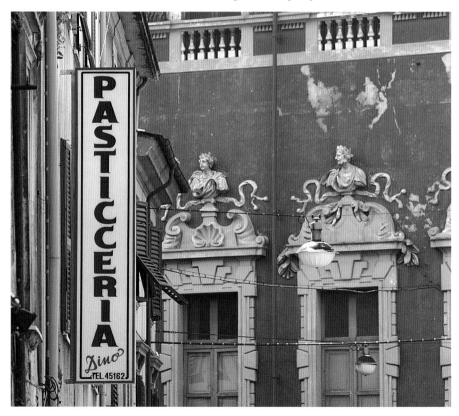

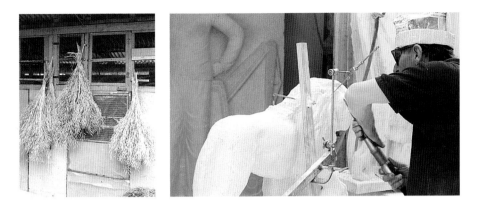

made principally from Vermentino, with 10–20 percent of the local grape Albarola. There are only about 20 hectares of vineyard in total. The view is dominated by the castle of the Malaspina, a powerful family which gained wealth by collecting tolls from the merchants and pilgrims using this once important trade route. Just past the bustling, prosperous town of Massa the hills are suddenly carpeted with a patchwork of vines. Seconds later they disappear just as suddenly, to be replaced by the quarried marble slopes of Carrara.

Carrara is an industrial, no-nonsense sort of town, stretching from the coast to the quarries. There is no sense of commemoration of the marble connection. Perhaps being surrounded by white slopes, thundering lorries and marble dust is enough. Just past Carrara the Colli di Luni wine zone begins. Red wines are made from about two-thirds Sangiovese, whites from Vermentino. Much of the zone is in the neighbouring coastal region of Liguria; the Tuscan part is inland. Almost immediately you see signs to the archaeological site of Luni itself on the left. This was the original Roman marble town, and the surrounding area is still called the Lunigiana. After about five minutes turn right to Fosdinovo, the centre of Tuscan Colli di Luni wine production, even though only about four hectares are planted.

Fosdinovo, the northernmost part of the route, is 500 metres high, as is much of the hilly road back to Carrara. Most is forested but there are areas of terracing and even dry-stone walls. The sad thing is how many vineyards have been abandoned. After about 20 minutes' descent into Carrara, a few vineyards appear (Candia dei Colli Apuani once more). The 'back road' from Carrara to Massa through the Alpi Apuane is hard to find (look for signs to Bergiola) but worth it for the natural beauty and to avoid the traffic. Once back in Massa, the next port of call is Lucca.

Above *The abundance of marble around Carrara is almost unworldy.* Below *Strips and patches of vine carpet the hills around Massa.* Far left *Massa is a working town rather than a tourist attraction, but it has a fair dose of civic pride.*

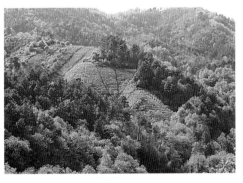

Il Passaggero
Massa, Via Alberica, 1
Tel: 0585 489651; cl. Sun, lunch Mon-Thu
Long-standing, inexpensive restaurant, in ancient building. Daily changing menu. Short range of local wines.
L'Enoteca
Carrara Marina, Viale Verrazzano, 11e
Tel: 0585 634420; cl. Sun
Ground floor enoteca, small restaurant beneath with wine-laden walls (700+ stocked). Snacks and full meals.

FOOD SHOPPING

Macelleria Galeotti
Massa, Via Aurelia Ovest
Top quality salumi.
Fornaio Dazzi
Carrara, Loc. Fossola
Bread, cakes, foccacia, baked on spot.
Gelateria Mario
Viareggio, Via Petrolini
Fruit-flavoured ice creams to die for.

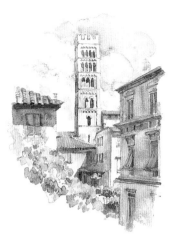

Lucca and environs

Lucca's encircling city walls, set behind a grassed-over moat and clutches of chestnut trees, will astonish. Low, thick and solid, they remain perfectly intact. Other ancient town walls, built taller but thinner, were knocked down during the 19th century when cities were rapidly expanding. Lucca's walls were rebuilt in the 16th century to survive attack and even town developers fought shy of dismantling them. As a result Lucca has changed very little (less even than Siena) and history oozes from every pore. Once an important Roman town, of which its neat grid of streets and Piazza Amfiteatro are reminders, Lucca became the medieval capital of Tuscany before gaining its independence and operating as a city state until 1799. Its economy was based on banking and the silk trade. Now it is better known as Tuscany's foremost olive oil town. Olive oil is also used liberally in its cuisine, as are the barley-like grain *farro* and chestnuts. So it is best to forget the waistline when eating there.

The area inside the walls is quite small, and easy to cover by foot. There are several splendid churches but the highlight is San Michele in the centre of town on the site of the old Roman forum.

Lucca is also the ideal base for touring the zones of Colline Lucchesi and Montecarlo.

LUCCA AND ENVIRONS

WINE PRODUCERS

Fattoria del Buonamico
Tel: 0583 22038; E, F
Montecarlo's most cited estate. Rosso di Cercatoia (Sangiovese/Syrah/Cabernet/Merlot) best known. Fruit-forward Montecarlo red and white.

Fattoria del Teso
Tel: 0583 286288; fax: 0583 287814; E, F
Up-and-coming, large Montecarlo estate. Clean, fresh, well-made wines. Range led by red Montecarlo Riserva L'Anfiteatro di Lucca. Visits afternoons only, booking not necessary. Book rooms with estate.

Tenuta di Valgiano
Tel & fax: 0583 402271; E, F
New estate, in north of zone, that has risen sharply from nowhere to become far and away Lucca's best. Rosso dei Palistorti (Sangiovese/Syrah/Merlot), Scasso dei Cesari

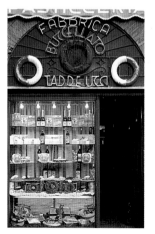

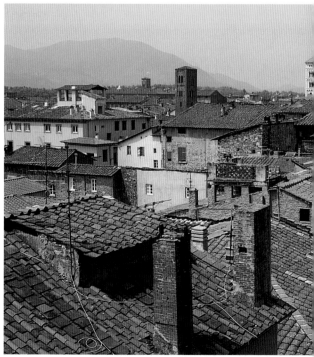

MONTECARLO

Montecarlo Rosso is an unexceptional mid-weight red, chiefly from Sangiovese with any or all of Canaiolo, Ciliegiolo, Colorino, Malvasia Nera, Syrah, Cabernet and others. There is as much choice with the white to enliven the basal Trebbiano: Sémillon, Pinot Grigio, Pinot Bianco, Vermentino, Sauvignon, Roussanne may all go into the pot. Nonetheless it is rare to find these varieties' flavours expressing themselves. Producers seem keener on the high-tech, light and tight approach.

Montecarlo is a tiny Medici village set atop a conical hill, its vineyards clustered around it in a compact, fairly densely planted zone. It takes about 20 minutes to reach the area from Lucca. Take the road to Altopascio (avoiding the motorway). Just past the large supermarket on the right near Porcari fork right (signed Altopascio) then immediately swing round left to Turchetto from where Montecarlo is signposted. You pass Fattoria del Buonamico on the right then, at the top of the incline: there is a right turn to the old centre. Turning left instead leads down past Fattoria Michi (on the left) and offers emblematic views. Continue down to the Lucca–Montecatini junction, and return to Lucca.

(Sangiovese), Giallo dei Muri (Trebbiano/Malvasia/Vermentino/Chardonnay) all impeccable. Pay for tastings. Must book. Book rooms with estate.

Le Murelle
Tel: 0583 394487
Small. Steep, well exposed vineyard. Concentrates on Sauvignon and Chardonnay: convinced Sangiovese is wrong for the area.

La Badiola
Tel: 0583 30633
Out on a limb at San Pancrazio (eastern wing). Uncomplicated, very drinkable wines.

ENOTECHE

Mini Montecarlo
Vanni Lucca
Vineria Marsili, Lucca
Marcucci Pietrasanta

EATING OUT

La Buca di Sant'Antonio
Lucca, Via della Cervia, 1
Tel: 0583 55881; cl. Sun eve, Mon

Below and left *Lucca's rooftops and a pasticceria.*
Right *Eagerly awaited each autumn are* funghi porcini.
Below right *Discarded demi-johns.*

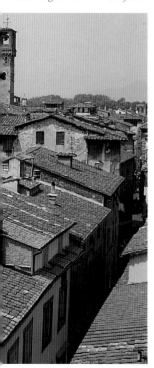

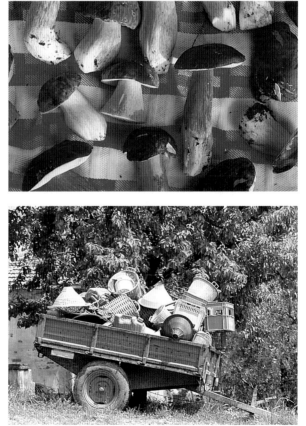

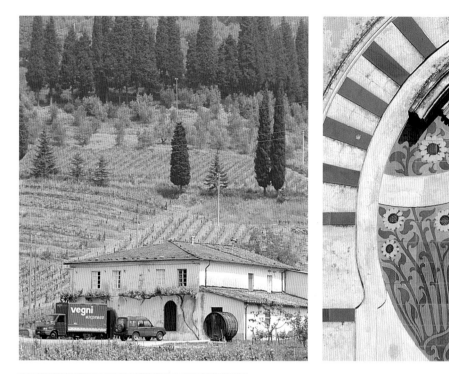

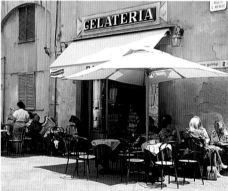

Top left *Vineyards criss-crossing the Colline Lucchesi.*
Above *A glorious example of art nouveau architecture on a palazzo façade in Lucca.*
Left *Enjoying ice cream at one of Lucca's* gelateria.
Right *This cheese shop also sells bread and wine.*

COLLINE LUCCHESI

Lucca's low hills rise like butterfly wings either side of the River Serchio that flows south towards the town. It is a comparatively rainy zone, the damp westerly air from the sea rising as it meets the hills and being pushed into black clouds. These are not good growing conditions for Sangiovese, and the DOC allows for a varietal Merlot and a low, 45–70 percent, Sangiovese blend as well as a varietal Sangiovese. Similarly, alongside a Trebbiano-based white is a varietal Sauvignon and a varietal Vermentino. Sadly, however, many producers are more enthusiastic than skilful and disappointing wines abound.

The western wing can be seen within half an hour. Leave Lucca on the road to Abetone, almost immediately turning left across the River Serchio towards Camaiore. At Cappella with the neatly ranked vineyards of Le Murelle on the right, turn back on yourself and then right at the third bridge over the Freddana stream – a matter of

The eating and meeting place for Lucca folk. Classic local dishes, fairly substantial. Firmly Tuscan wine list.
Puccini
Lucca, Corte San Lorenzo, 1
Tel: 0583 316116; cl. Tue
Attractive, welcoming, good quality fish restaurant. Reasonable wine list. Seats outside. Fairly costly.
Il Mecenate
Lucca, Loc. Gattaiola, Via della Chiesa, 707
Tel: 0583 512167; cl. Mon
In converted old stables. Local foods, seasonally changing menu. Home made pasta, desserts. Not costly.

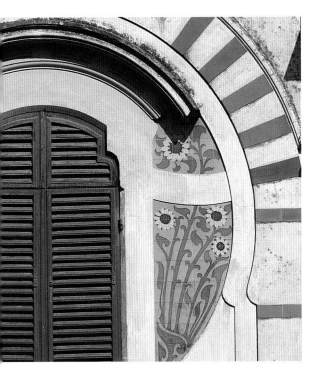

Alla Taverna di Mario
Montecarlo, Piazza Carrara, 12-13
Tel: 0583 22588; cl. Mon
Family-run. Good quality local
ingredients. Seasonally changing menu.
Classic dishes. Fine meats. Local and
regional wines. Good value.

Forino
Capannori, Via Piaggia, 13
Tel: 0583 935302; cl. Sun eve, Mon
Family-run restaurant. Mainly fish-based.
Carefully chosen wines, helpful service.
Seats outside. Very good value.

HOTELS

Locanda L'Elisa
Lucca, Fraz. Massa Pisana, SS.12.bis
del Brennero, 1952
Tel: 0583 379737; fax: 0583 379019
5* Relais & Châteaux in old
Napoleonic villa. Large, elegant, stylish
rooms; good bathrooms. Garden, pool.
Facilities for tennis, golf, horseriding.
On-site restaurant. Parking.

Villa La Principessa
Lucca, Fraz. Massa Pisana, SS.12.bis
del Brennero, 1616
Tel: 0583 370037; fax: 0583 379136
In early 19th-century villa. Country
house atmosphere. Gardens. Pool.
Parking. 4*

Piccolo Puccini
Lucca, Via di Poggio, 9
Tel: 0583 55421; fax: 0583 53487
In old centre, by church. Small
Renaissance building. Attractive
rooms. Good service. Garage. 3*.

seconds – to Mutigliano. Just before the church on the right, turn left and amble down to Monte San Quirico and back to Lucca.

The Abetone road is also the starting point for the eastern wing. Branch right onto a tiny road to Pescia. Most of the views are to the right as the road cuts through at high level, overlooking an amphitheatre of vines and olives. Just past Matraia is a lay-by from where to survey the whole scene. (The pink buildings down to the right belong to Fattoria Colleverde.) After about ten minutes of slow driving take the right turn to Camigliano. Make sure you see the superlative Villa Torrigiani before turning left again to Tofori. You pass Fattoria Maionchi on the right, from where signs lead to Fattoria di Fubbiano. You can then turn back to Lucca or proceed eastward into the zone of Bianco della Valdinievole (see p130).

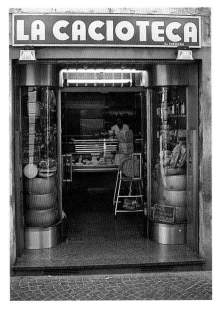

BIANCO DELLA VALDINIEVOLE
WINE PRODUCERS

Fattoria di Montellori
Fucechio
Tel: 0571 242625
Numerous plots, diverse
characteristics, over large area. Wide
range of characterful wines.
Le Calvane
Montespertoli, Loc. Montagnana Val
di Pesa
Tel & fax: 0571 671073; E
Chunky, reliable wines. Large range.
Visits working hours only. May pay for
tastings. Book rooms with estate or
agency several months prior.
Fattoria Castello Sonnino
Montespertoli
Tel: 0571 609198; E, F, G
Largish estate. Two Chianti
Montespertoli: Fattoria Sonnino
(Sangiovese/Canaiolo/Trebbiano/Malva
sia), Castello di Montespertoli (90%
Sangiovese/10% Canaiolo); others.
May pay for tastings. Must book.

ENOTECHE

Wine Club Pescia

EATING OUT

Cecco
Pescia, Via Forti, 96
Tel: 0572 477955; cl. Mon
Long-standing, sound restaurant.
Traditional dishes, fish- and meat-based.
Pescia asparagus. Fair regional wine list.
Monte a Pescia
Monte a Pescia, Via del Monte Ovest, I
Tel: 0572 476887; cl. Wed
Wide range of meats cooked over an
open fire. Other Tuscan dishes. Short
wine range, good house.
Cucina da Giovanni
Enoteca Giovanni
Montecatini Terme, Via Garibaldi 25/27
Tel: 0572 71695; cl. Mon
Confusingly 'Enoteca' is the
restaurant, 'Cucina' the wine bar.
Well-flavoured, local foods from good
ingredients. Huge choice of wines.
Seats outside. Slightly costly.
La Taverno dell'Ozio
San Miniato, Loc. Corazzano, Via Zara, 85
Tel: 0571 462862; cl. Sun lunch, Wed
Good, robust Tuscan classics, packed
with flavour in easy-going trattoria.
Pizzas too. Fair range of regional
wines. Cheap.

Lucca to Florence

BIANCO DELLA VALDINIEVOLE

The Nievole River valley runs along the eastern edge of this area, not through its heartland around Cozzile. Vineyards appear in occasional clumps, well separated, although there is quite a lot of abandoned terracing. The wine, mainly from Trebbiano, is light, crisp, sometimes a little fizzy and unexceptional; most is drunk locally. There is also a Vin Santo. The production area, however, is diverse, visually wonderful, quite different from other parts of Tuscany and well deserving of the couple of hours it takes to see it properly.

If you are coming from Lucca, head for Pescia, joining the route at the Collodi turn-off; if from the Colline Lucchesi, through the glorious, olive-drenched scenery of Petrognano and San Gennaro. From there take the road downward (if in doubt, turn left), overlooking the reservoirs of the plain below, eventually following a sign to Collodi across the valley.

Next make for Pescia, known for its flower nurseries and asparagus, where there is a choice. If you feel brave, cross the river, then fork left and head towards Malocchio. The road rapidly declines to a narrow, rutted track but forms a pretty short-cut to Cozzile. For a gentler journey and fine panoramas, do not cross the river but continue northward towards Vellano. After a little lowish land along the narrow river valley (rather like Chianti Rufina), the road zig-zags up through dense pine forests that blanket the precipitous slopes. From the northernmost extreme there are fine views over the lower land. You may also see the 2,000m peak of Mount Cimone, about 25 kilometres away.

Twist down, back into olive grove punctuated by occasional vines, to Cozzile, Massa (another one) and the outskirts of Montecatini. There branch left, reascending to Vico, then to Serravalle Pistoiese, before swinging back along and under

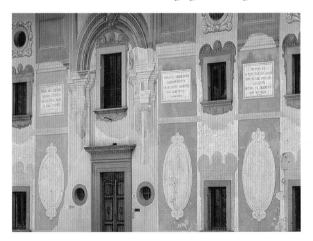

Right The stunning façade of the Palazzo Vescovile in San Miniato, on the edge of the Colline Pisane.

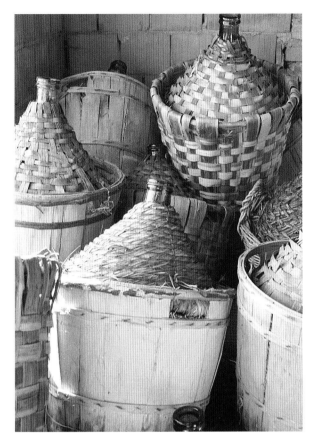

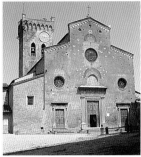

Above *An ancient church in the wonderful castellated village of San Miniato.*
Left *Old-fashioned wicker-encased bottles of Bianco dell'Empolese.*

L'Artevino
Montespertoli, Via Sonnino, 28
Tel: 0571 608488; cl. Wed
Small, elegant place. Attractive local dishes, cooked with care. Good desserts. Carefully chosen wines.

Il Focolare
Montespertoli, Loc. Montagnana, Via Volterra Nord, 173
Tel: 0571 671132; cl. Mon eve, Tue
Go for the huge fiorentina steaks and other substantial Tuscan fare. Regional wine list. Seats outside. Inexpensive.

La Panzanella
Empoli, Via dei Cappuccini, 10
Tel: 0571 922182; cl. Sat lunch, Sun
Wonderful homely cooking, absolutely classic dishes. Small, mainly local wine list, good house. Seats outside. Good value.

SPAS

Montecatini Terme
The town oozes wealth, vigour and glitz. There are smart bars, restaurants and hotels, bustle and bright lights. The spa itself is huge and supremely elegant, with marble avenues fronting the treatment areas and much ceremony surrounding the dispensing of its waters.

Monsummano Terme
Wide range of treatments but, for full benefit, go underground in the Grotta Giusti, where the hot springs emerge through a submerged lake.

FOOD SHOPPING

Pasticceria Bargilli Viale Grocco
Pasticceria Desideri Via Gorizia Montecatini Terme. The places for Montecatini's own sweetmeat, *cialde*, sliced almonds and sugar enclosed in a pair of wafers.

the motorway to Monsummano. This leads through the southern spur of the area which has completely different countryside: open, flattish, and intensively cultivated.

BIANCO DELL'EMPOLESE / MONTESPERTOLI

Between Puntone and Stabbia the road crosses into the pretty Bianco dell'Empolese area. Empoli's wines are made chiefly from Trebbiano, with some Vin Santo too. The zone is more extensive than Valdinievole but all the vineyards of any merit are concentrated around Fucecchio to the south. So continue along the same road for ten to 15 minutes to . Before long you see increasing numbers of vines draped graciously across the hills until, approaching Fucecchio, they surround you completely.

From Fucecchio cross the river Arno to see the castellated jewel of San Miniato and onward to Montespertoli, a Chianti sub-zone. Then return to Empoli, a large commercial town. Heading along the river, the low slopes of Empoli's hills form a backdrop to its wine zone. With its neat fields and square-towered villas the scene starts to look more like central Tuscany, and a sense of well-being hangs in the air.

CARMIGNANO

WINE PRODUCERS

Tenuta di Capezzana
Tel: 055 8706005; E, F
Run by the family of the amiable Count
Ugo Contini Bonacossi, this estate
continues to set the pace in
Carmignano with its range of supremely
fine wines. Villa di Trefiano run by son
Vittorio. Book rooms with estate.

Artimino
Tel: 055 8792051
Huge estate, concentrating on reds.
Wines have improved notably recently.

Il Poggiolo
Tel: 055 8711242
Slow-maturing wines gaining attention.

Fattoria Ambra
Tel: 055 8719049
Sound quality. Three cru versions of
Carmignano: Santa Cristina in Pilli, Le
Vigne Alte, Elzana.

Tenuta Cantagallo
Capraia e Limite
Tel: 0571 910078; E
Vineyards in Chianti Classico and
Montalbano as well as Carmignano.
Dense, well-structured wines with
individuality. Notable Carleto (Riesling
Renano). Visits working hours only.

Tenuta di Bagnolo
Montemurlo
Tel: 0574 652439; E, F, G
An oddity. Owned by Marquis Vittorio
Pancrazi. Situated in a non-viney area
between Prato and Pistoia and makes
only intense, powerful Villa di Bagnolo,
from 100% Pinot Nero. Wine
renowned and widely admired.
Must book.

Right *The tiny village of
Carmignano has some delightful old
features such as this alcoved wall.*

Carmignano

Carmignano is a small zone bounded by the Prato plain and the high Mount Albano which gives its name to the overlapping Chianti Montalbano zone. Carmignano lies in Monte Albano's rain shadow and benefits from cool air from its slopes, giving better growing conditions than further west.

The wine, DOCG, is from one of the first demarcated zones – defined in 1716. It was also the first denomination to permit Cabernet Sauvignon in its Chianti-esque blend, due to Count Ugo Contini Bonacossi of the Capezzana estate, who managed to convince the DOC committee that, since the Cabernet had most likely been brought to the area from France by the Medicis 200 years prior, it was as 'traditional' as any grape in the area. DOC committees eventually allowed Cabernet in the blend.

Carmignano is distinguished by its elegance and finesse. The best, marked by an almost perfect balance, live for decades

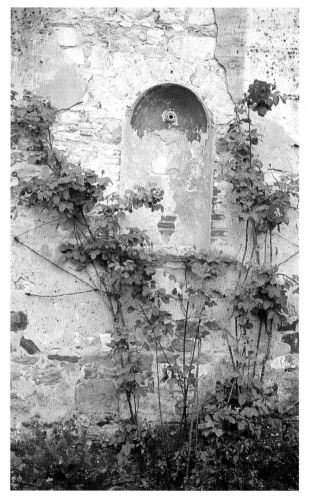

although are drinkable almost from day one. A lighter style, is also made, named Barco Reale di Carmignano DOC after a long Medici boundary wall which still stands. There is also a rosé 'Vinruspo', Vin Santo and red Vin Santo Occhio di Pernice.

Carmignano can be reached easily from both Empoli or Florence. In either case make for Lastra a Signa or Signa to reach Ponte a Signa, which crosses the Arno. Once north of the river, turn left, and follow a slim road along its north bank. After a few minutes, follow a sign to the right to Artimino. This marks the beginning of the zone. Wind upwards past well tended vines to the walled hamlet of Artimino. The villa, once a Medici hunting lodge, and its adjacent hotel and restaurant complex are just outside the tiny village. From there, amble through peaceful, vine-clad scenery to La Serra and on to Carmignano itself, near the vineyards of Il Poggiolo. Next head for Santa Cristina (direction Vinci) with wonderful views back eastwards over Florence. You may even be able to pick out the Duomo.

Past Santa Cristina the road begins to rise onto the pine-clad slopes of Monte Albano. Just as you think you have left the zone well behind, there is a road to the right (not on most maps) that takes you to Bacchereto. It skirts under the mountain for a couple of kilometres and brings you onto the second side of Carmignano's saddle-like formation.

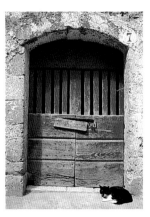

EATING OUT

Da Delfina
Carmignano, Loc. Artimino
Tel: 055 8718074; cl. Mon eve, Tue
Elegant, well-appointed restaurant, attentive to detail. Menu varies seasonally, good use of vegetables throughout traditionally-based meal. Local and national wines. Eat on terrace in summer. Not overly costly.

Su Pe' I Canto
Carmignano, Piazza Matteotti, 25-26
Tel: 055 8712490; cl. Mon
Small place with good atmosphere. Go just for one dish or a full meal: flavoursome Tuscan classics, simple and nourishing. Great choice of wines, local and regional.

Il Castagno di Pier Angelo
Pistoia, Loc. Castagno di Piteccio
Tel: 0573 42214; eves only, cl. Mon
Hard to find but worth the effort. Fine, intriguing dishes based on local ingredients. Good desserts. Tasting menus (fish-based and meat-based). Very well balanced wine list. Great value throughout.

Lo Storno
Pistoia, Via del Lastrone, 8
Tel: 0573 26193; cl. Sun
Ancient hostelry in medieval times. All effort goes into the flavoursome, frequently changing primi and main courses. Otherwise just simple desserts, one cheese, one wine (well chosen). Cash only. Cheap.

Enoteca Barni
Prato, Via Ferrucci, 24

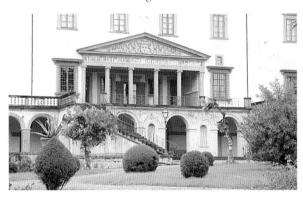

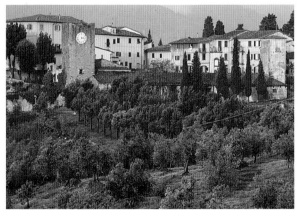

Above left *The large villa just outside the tiny village of Artimino (left) was used by the Medicis as a hunting lodge. There is now a hotel/restaurant complex alongside.*
Top *Grandeur mixes with rustic in Artimino.*

Tel: 0574 607845; cl. Mon lunch, Sun
Despite name, refined restaurant.
Beautifully original dishes yet grounded
in Tuscan roots. Wide-ranging wine
list. Remarkably good value.
La Vecchia Cucina
Prato, Via Pomeria, 23
Tel: 0574 34665; cl. Sun
Friendly, traditional-style trattoria.
Unfussy, good Tuscan food, full of
flavour. Shortish but reliable wine list.
Cash only. Great value.

HOTELS

Paggeria Medicea
Carmignano, Loc. Artimino
Tel: 055 8718081; fax: 055 8718080
On Artimino estate. Medici villa,
furnished with antiques. Well
appointed rooms. Pool, fitness track,
tennis courts. Parking. High level 4*
Hermitage
Poggio a Caiano
Tel: 055 877244; fax: 055 8797057
Comfortable, modern, friendly. Pool.
Parking. 3*.

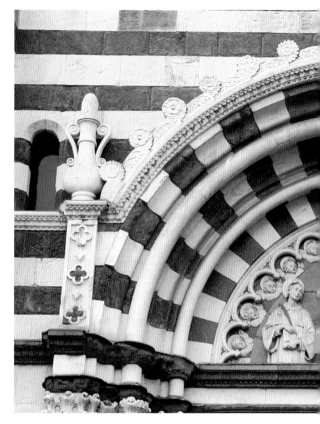

Main picture *Pistoia's striking
striped Cathedral of San Zeno.*
Below and far right *Relaxing in
the bars and restaurants of Pistoia.*
Bottom *The colourful old hospital
frieze, one of several treasures in this
elegant town.*

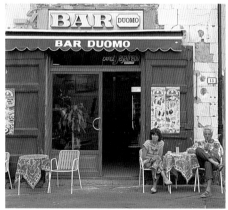

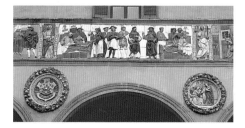

From Bacchereto, the area's top estate,
Capezzana, is signed. Skirt past the villa of
Bacchereto (detour left to see the estate),
then follow the road through the hillside,
with Florence in front of you. Just when
you think the city is so close you must have
come too far, you pass a tiny chapel, then
the cellars (both right), and estate buildings
(left) of Capezzana. Twist down the narrow, cypress-lined avenue back to reality
and the rather mundane village of Seano.

You could now pass through Poggio a
Caiano, where Fattoria Ambra is based, to
return to Florence, or take the motorway.
But first it is well worth taking a look at
the well-heeled towns of Pistoia and Prato.

PISTOIA

Just 20 minutes from Seano, Pistoia is an
elegant place with smart shops and a quiet
hum of people going about their business.
Of Roman origin and later important as a
banking centre, it was frequently bounced

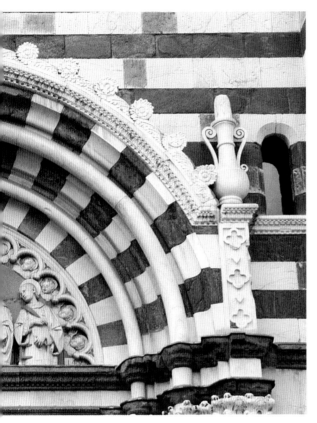

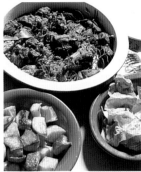

between continually warring Florence and Lucca and suffered accordingly. Its solid city walls and gates contain the Piazza del Duomo, with its green and white striped Cathedral of San Zeno, bell tower and baptistery. Pistoians think the Florentine hordes are stupid to miss their town's splendours – visitors tend to agree. And it is certainly nicer browsing the elegant shops in peace and no souvenir shops interrupting the stylish displays of Italian chic.

PRATO

Approached through a dreary mass of industrial sprawl (the road via Montale is the least dull), Prato has the industrious feel of a bustling northern city. It has been famous for textiles since the 12th century, and they are still its major industry and a continuing source of wealth. Almost as famous are the *biscotti di Prato*, long, crunchy almond biscuits like *cantucci* that are often dunked in Vin Santo. The solid city walls of the medieval centre and the rugged 13th-century Norman-style castle (the only one in Tuscany) reflect the town's hard-working atmosphere.

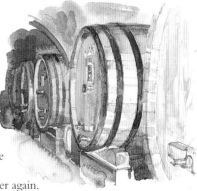

Now go safely back to Florence – and start all over again.

GLOSSARY

Alberese – limestone soil, renowned for vineyards in Chianti Classico

Acquavite – spirit, distilled from grapes or other fruit

Affinamento – keeping newly-bottled wine before release, to soften it a little

Alimentari – small, general food store

Aurelia (Via) – the first main state road, the SS1, built by Mussolini. Follows the coast from Rome to the French border. Successive constructions now give a choice of a 'new' or an 'old' Aurelia as well as a motorway in places. Often referred to in speech and on road signs

Autostrada – motorway, tolls are payable

Azienda – estate

Azienda agricola, azienda agraria – estate making wine from own grapes

Azienda vinicola – estate making wine from bought-in grapes

Azienda vitivinicola – estate making wine from both own and bought-in grapes

Barrique – small oak wine cask, most commonly of 225 litres, sometimes 500, made from French oak and used either new or up to the third year of age. Not traditional but increasingly common.

Botte (pl botti) – traditional wine cask, usually of Slavonian oak, large (25hl plus) and kept for many years

Bruschetta (pl bruschette) – toasted Tuscan bread, rubbed with garlic and drenched in olive oil; may also come with tomatoes, black cabbage or other topping

Cacioteria – unusual, local terminology for cheese shop

Campanile – bell tower

Cantina Sociale (pl cantine sociali) – cooperative winemaking and/or bottling cellar

Cantucci/cantuccini – hard, crispy biscuits with almond slivers, best dunked into Vin Santo

Caratelli – small casks, typically about 50 litres, used for maturing Vin Santo

Casa colonica (pl case coloniche) – traditional farmworker's house

Cassia (Via) – the second main state road, the SS2, leading from Rome, through Siena to Florence (see also Aurelia)

Chiantigiana – the road that cuts right through Chianti Classico

Classico – the central, classic heart-land of any wine zone; usually classico wines are better than non-classico (called normale)

Colli (sing colle) – hills

Colline (sing collina) – small hills

Comune – commune or parish; smallest self-governing geographical unit

Consorzio (pl consorzi) – a voluntary body set up to protect its members' interests; controls standards, and assists with marketing strategies.

Cru – unofficial but frequently used term for wine from single vineyard

Enoteca (pl enoteche) – wine shop; often used also to mean winebar or wine shop with tastings Enoiteca – official word for wine shop with tastings, infrequently used

Fagioli – white kidney beans

Farro – a barley-like grain, used in soups and first courses

Fattoria – farm or estate (factory is **fabbrica**)

Fiaschetteria – old fashioned Florentine term for wine shop

Frantoio – olive oil crushing and pressing plant

Frazione – literally fraction; part of a commune or parish with its own name and identity

Frizzante –lightly sparkling

Fiume – river

Galestro – clay-schist soil important for quality in Chianti Classico

Gastronomia – delicatessen, also sells prepared dishes

Governo – traditional practice, once almost abandoned, now staging a comeback, in making Chianti; some grapes are held back, then added to the just-fermented wine later to restart the fermentation; benefits/drawbacks disputed

Grappa – spirit made from grape lees (qv)

Hectare (Ha) – measurement of area, about 2.47 acres

Hectolitre (Hl) – 100 litres

La Fiorentina – a large, T-bone steak, usually for two people and a great speciality

Lees – mass of skins and stalks left after a wine's fermentation

Località – small locality, similar to Frazione (qv)

Macelleria – butcher

Maceration – seeping of grape skins in the grape juice

Mercatino – flea market

Mercato – market

Mezzadria – old crop-sharing system

Must – grape juice

Normale – non-Riserva wine (qv)

Panetteria – bread shop

Passeggiata – common Tuscan (and Italian) practice of going for a stroll in the early evening; more than a leg-stretch it's an important people-watching, mating and gossip-gathering occasion; each town has own, never-changing times and routes

Passito – wine made from dried or semi-dried grapes

Pasticceria – pastry shop

Pecorino – ewe's milk cheese

Pizzicheria – local Florentine term for *gastronomia* (qv)

Podere (*pl* poderi) – small farm or plot

Provincia – province, administrative unit between regione and commune (qv)

Quintale (*pl* quintali) – unit of weight, equal to 100 kilos

Regione – region, largest Italian administrative unit; there are 20 of which Tuscany is one

Resa – yield of volume of grape must expressed as a percentage of grape weight, most commonly 70%

Ribollita – a soup based on vegetables cooked at length, thickened with bread

Riserva – wine, usually from a better year or a particular selection of grapes, aged longer than normal. Minimum

length of ageing is controlled by wine law and differs from wine to wine.

Salumeria – shop selling salumi (see below)

Salumi – cured meats: salami, prosciutto etc, and occasionally fish (salt cod, anchovies and the like)

Sformato – a type of vegetable mousse, often served as a main course accompaniment

S.P. – strada provinciale, provincial road; each province has own numbering system

S.S. – strada statale, state road; one system of numbering throughout Italy

Sulphur dioxide (SO2) – an antioxidant of necessity used in all wine; undetectable and harmless if quantities carefully restricted

Superstrada – fast, toll-free, dual carriageway road

Torrente – small stream, often no more than a trickle but subject to occasional surges

Varietà – grape variety

Varietal – a grape variety

Vin Santo – a (usually) sweet wine made from grapes left to dry for about three months after the harvest

Vintage – harvest; the year the wine was made

GAZETTEER

INDEX

Indexer's note: Towns are given in brackets for hotels and restaurants

PICTURE CREDITS

ACKNOWLEDGEMENTS

Other people's acknowledgements are hardly ever of great interest and from time to time I've wondered why authors didn't just thank the people personally and leave it at that. But I didn't realise how much the help of people along the way matters when writing a book, how they can make the seemingly impossible happen and, vitally, how they can keep your morale topped up. It was also a source of amazement and pleasure that so many people were willingly prepared to offer so much time and expertise, often at very short notice, even those for whom the project can bring no benefit at all. It would be unthinkable not to acknowledge such magnificent assistance publicly and permanently. So I abundantly thank:

Ursula Thurner, Consorzio del Marchio Storico, who started me off, set the tone, made me realise the scope and that it was attainable, who was assiduous in the preparation and execution of her days with me and opened my eyes to so much;
Bruno & Elyane Moos, whose weekend I ruined, whom I totally exhausted but who still kept smiling - and came back for more. They made an ace Directory Enquiries service too. I don't know what I'd have done without them;
Christine, who gives new meaning to the sound of a cockerel, who deserves a very long list of thank yous but instead will be rewarded by a return trip to Livorno for drawing the short straw;
Liz, who sacrificed the tastings she was hoping for to cover all the wine-free bits and who made all the hard work fun;
Giuseppe Mazzocolin, who was continually interrupted by innumerable faxes from me but answered them anyway, whom I managed not to see three times in succession, who was plagued by misfortune in getting me certain documentation but who was still invaluable;
Francesco Giuntini, who will be terribly disgruntled that he's not mentioned first in this list but will at least be relieved to know he's in front of Ugo Contini who never batted an eyelid when I turned up at incredibly short notice and who succinctly filled me in on Carmignano in his usual efficient, charming manner.
Faith Heller-Willinger whose support and advice at the end of a phone line gave eating in Tuscany a new perspective.
Franca Spinola, President, Camera di Commerzio IAA di Grosseto;
Roberto Saletti, Camera di Commerzio IAA Grosseto;
Giacomo Regina, Camera di Commerzio IAA Grosseto;
Valter Nunziatini, Amm Reg Provincia di Grosseto, Giovanni Prisco, AIS;
Paolo Solini, Consorzio Vino Nobile di Montepulciano, who covered an amazing amount of ground in exhaustive detail,
Stefano Campatelli, Consorzio Brunello di Montalcino, as ever diligent, detailed and enthusiastic and with the rare skill of making a tough, unenviable task seem a pleasure.
Marie-Sylvie Haniez-Melosi, Movimento Nazionale del Turismo di Vino, who not only provided some incredibly useful pointers but, with her husband Roberto, gave me one of the most fun evenings I've had in Italy in a long time;
Paolo Valdastri, literary life-saver of Livorno;
Angelica Faguioli, who set me straight on San Gimignano;
Maria Pia Maionchi, for relaxed hospitality and comprehensive information on Lucca;
My parents, they'll know why;
Plus all the Gamberi and Arcigolosi who, unknowingly, pointed me in the right directions for good eating places and food and all the other people who, knowingly or not, got me through.
Above all, a big thank you to Stephanie for the editorial support I'd so often heard about but never before experienced and to Sue for stepping magnificently into the breach.

ACKNOWLEDGEMENTS FOR THE REVISED EDITION

With great thanks to all the producers who responded so promptly for requests for additional information, despite the difficult time of year, and to Lucy for pulling it all together.

PUBLISHERS OF AGRITOURISM GUIDES

Agriturist
Corso Vittorio Emanuele 101, 00186 Rome
Tel: 0039 06 6852353
Fax: 0039 06 68307981

Terranostra
Via XXIV Maggio 43, 00187 Rome
Tel: 0039 06 4682370
Fax: 0039 06 4682204
terranostra@coldiretti.it
www.terranostra.it

Panorama "Turismo Verde"

Mondadori

Italia Agritur
SS Sublacense km 13.600, 00028 Subiaco (RM)
Tel: 0039 0774 84900/822434
Fax: 0039 0774 84170
iter@mclink.it

Demeter
Via Strà 167, SS11, 37030 Cologna ai Colli (VR)
Tel: 0039 045 6174111
Fax: 0039 045 6174100